JUGGER

The German Way of Business: Why
It Is Transforming Europe—
and the World

SIMON & SCHUSTER

NAUT

PHILIP
GLOUCHEVITCH

New York London Toronto Sydney Tokyo Singapore

SIMON & SCHUSTER
Simon & Schuster Building
Rockefeller Center
1230 Avenue of the Americas
New York, New York 10020

Designed by Caroline Cunningham

Manufactured in the United States of America

1   2   3   4   5   6   7   8   9   10

Library of Congress Cataloging-in-Publication Data
Glouchevitch, Philip.
Juggernaut : the German way of business : why it is transforming Europe—
and the world / Philip Glouchevitch.
p.   cm.
Includes bibliographical references and index.
1. Industrial management—Germany.   2. Germany—Economic policy.
3. Germany—Foreign economic relations—Europe.   4. Europe—Foreign
economic relations—Germany.   5. Competition, International.
I. Title.
HD70.G2G58   1992
338.943—dc20   92-19015
CIP
ISBN 0-671-74410-0

The excerpt from Stephen Bepler's speech, on pages 52–53, is reprinted, with
permission, from *Investing Worldwide,* copyright 1990, Association for Investment
Management and Research, Charlottesville, Virginia.

The excerpt on pages 138–39 from Reinhard Mohn's *Success Through Partnership*
is reprinted by permission of the publisher, Doubleday, a division of Doubleday,
Dell Publishing Group, Inc.

CONTENTS

PREFACE

In the aftermath of German reunification and on the eve of Europe's push toward increasing economic and political integration, the face of German business is changing rapidly, yet its soul stays much the same. German business is indeed a kind of unstoppable force—the "juggernaut" of the title: its highly skilled labor force, its cautious and determined business ethic, its powerful and controversial banking system have served the country extremely well in the course of its postwar "economic miracle." While we should not view German business as a menacing power determined to destroy everything in its path, it would be naive for Americans to ignore the fact that the Japanese are not the only economic threat we face. We do ourselves a disservice to ignore Germany's increasing economic—and political—power.

The purpose of this book is to examine in some detail the nature of the soul of German business. It does not attempt to chronicle fully all the latest changes, the mergers, the strategies, the opportunities won and lost; that task is better left up to newspapers and magazines. Instead, this book takes a step back to look at the ways of German business right now. The salient characteristics of Germany's business success—the apprenticeship system, the role of the small and medium-size companies known collectively as the *Mittelstand,* the "universal" banking system and others—make up the real subject of this book. Without an understanding of these central features of how business gets done in Germany, you won't know much about Germany, and you won't know much about its extraordinarily successful economy.

The approach I have taken throughout this book is decidedly microeconomic and practical. As such, it is neither a textbook on theoretical management nor a work of business mysticism designed to convert the world to The German Way. Rather, I prefer to see it as a kind of guide through the complex and often closed world of German business, both for those who really need such a guide in their own work and for those who are just curious. As much as possible, I try to capture that world through the firsthand experience of people who work in or with German business.

The picture that emerges from their stories is both encouraging and a cause for caution for many Germans. German business has been remarkably successful in finding a balance between social concerns and economic growth: capitalism with a human face. But it's important to remember that Germany's business success was accomplished in the context of the country's postwar economic miracle, when Germans were forced to rely on themselves to rebuild their country—with more than a little financial help from the United States. And that success remains limited to Germany itself. Germany now faces challenges extending beyond the borders of the former western sector: to rebuild eastern Germany and to help in the slow and no doubt painful process of drawing Europe into a single economic entity. Both tasks involve finding ways of accommodating different business cultures and making them mesh together—still uncharted territory for a notoriously insular business mentality.

At present, German business remains extremely private. Even the large public corporations prefer to play things close to the vest, and management tends to go its own way without much regard to outside influences such as corporate ownership. Whether German corporations can play the game more openly while maintaining their strong economic position as well as their social concern remains to be seen. And it is undoubtedly the key question for the coming decade.

I would be remiss if I did not thank several people who helped me with this book.

My agents, Linda Chester and Laurie Fox, spared no efforts to ensure that this book would see the light of day. Edward Baker did a tremendous job of editing and organizing the manuscript so that others might be able to read it. Joachim Luerman offered tremendous insight into the world of German business, which he knows so well. My editor at Simon & Schuster, Fred Hills, has remained patient and confident throughout.

I must also thank Christoph Schoeller (wise beyond his years), Margaret Talcott, Dietrich Solaro, Knut Bleicher and Nick Wolff. And "meine liebe" Laura Byrne; one of the privileges of authorship lies in getting the chance to thank one's spouse publicly for all the support and encouragement, and I gladly take this opportunity to do so.

One final note. In the interest of accuracy, I have left all deutsche mark figures in their original denomination. As this book goes to press, one deutsche mark is worth about $.60.

1

Germany:
Yesterday and Today

Stand atop the Zugspitze, Germany's highest point, and look
to the north. The view is postcard-perfect: the high alpine snows
on the craggy peaks melt at the lower elevations, where torrents
dive into the dark green pine forests. In the distance, the Bavarian
farmland, with its contrasting greens of field and forest, rolls
toward the valley of the Danube. Nestled among the hills and
fields, the occasional village reveals its onion-domed church. The
scene has a timeless quality; nothing seems to have changed since
the Middle Ages.

Down in the valleys and cities, however, time is by no means
standing still. The Germans are engaged in a unique, double-sided

historical experiment. On the one hand, the battle that divided Germany between communism and capitalism, democracy and socialism, has become a struggle to see how quickly and painlessly the capitalist, democratic West can buy up and convert the communist, socialist East. On the other, Germany has taken the economic—if not political—lead in the ongoing attempts to create a unified Europe.

Forty-five Years after the Miracle

With Europe's biggest economy, its largest population and a pivotal location on the Continent, Germany is more than ever at the heart of Europe.

In 1991, the German economy drew in DM 335 billion in imports from other European Community members and pumped back another DM 360 billion in exports. In absolute terms, Germany runs neck and neck with the United States and ahead of Japan as the world's leading exporter, even though the German economy is only one quarter the size of the United States'. With a few local exceptions—trade between Ireland and Britain or Portugal and Spain—Germany is the leading trading partner for every other member of the EC. Germany also leads all Western countries in trading with the old Comecon countries of Eastern Europe.

A glance at the map of Europe confirms the preeminent location of Germany in "Mitteleuropa." From the Black Forest in the south, the headwaters of the Danube flow east through the lands of the old Hapsburg and Ottoman empires—Austria, Czechoslovakia, Hungary, Yugoslavia, Romania, and Bulgaria—and out to the Black Sea. Back in Germany and one watershed over from the Danube is the mighty Rhine. Historically one of Europe's most important commercial waterways, the Rhine links Germany's industrial heartland with Switzerland, France, the Netherlands and the port of Rotterdam on the North Sea. In 1992, the new Rhine-Danube canal opens, thus connecting the two great rivers and creating a waterborne trade route extending all the way from the North Sea to the Black, and from there to the Mediterranean.

In many ways, Germany has become a model country for the rest of Europe and for the world: wealth without much poverty, industrialization with concern for the environment. Look hard at the Ruhr Valley, where the downturn in the once-proud German coal and steel industry caused high unemployment in the 1970s, and you might find some urban decay—but not much. The Ruhr has succeeded in attracting new businesses, and many of the old ones have diversified into more promising fields. The hinterlands of Bavaria near the Czech border hide some depressed rural regions—but Appalachia should be so poor. Indeed, no single part of Germany functions as the equivalent of, say, New York, Tokyo, London or Paris. The big German banks are all in Frankfurt, but the headquarters of the large industrial corporations are spread out among a number of large cities—Munich, Stuttgart, Cologne, Düsseldorf, Hamburg, Berlin—and many smaller ones.

Germany's infrastructure is second to none in Europe. Consider the country's exemplary highway system: most people think of the German Autobahn as the natural habitat of Porsches and Mercedeses moving at 220 kilometers per hour—not entirely false, but often the highways are clogged with enough commercial trucking to make such high speeds impossible. And the highway system has not come at the expense of mass transit, as it has in the United States. The German government has invested heavily in developing its own high-speed rail system so as not to be left behind by the French and the Japanese.

Of course, Germany has not been entirely free of problems, even before it absorbed its eastern counterpart. Unemployment averaged over 6 percent for most of the 1980s, only slightly better than the U.S. average of around 7 percent—although unemployed Germans are much better provided for. At one point, the German government offered "guest workers"—primarily Turks, but also Yugoslavs, Romanians, Czechs, Poles and other Eastern Europeans—cash incentives to return home, the logic being that such payments would be cheaper than extended unemployment benefits. For those guest workers who stayed, acceptance into German society has often been difficult, as the recent violent outbursts by neo-Nazi skinheads demonstrate.

Reunification has created more problems for Germany. The high unemployment levels in the East—over 17 percent in 1992 —the need to restructure entire industries, the ghastly pollution, all have been well publicized. But there are sociological problems as well. East German women were accustomed to working and having child care provided by the state. Laws on abortion were much more liberal in the East. The list is long, and the two regions' problems and differences are not being solved as fast as some would like.

Curiously, until it actually occurred, no one in West Germany really believed the reunification of the two Germanies would ever come about, and most West Germans were perfectly happy without it. The population had adapted well to the narrowed confines of the country, which was not much more than half the size of the prewar state: a scant thirty miles across near Hamburg, with a fragile lifeline into encircled Berlin. With the unprecedented prosperity of the western zone, who needed the East? Yet despite the lack of interest, the "German question" lingered in the minds of many West Germans. How could the Germans ignore the frequent U.S. or French or British warplanes roaring a few thousand feet above their houses? How could they forget the missiles aimed at their country from both sides: the Soviet SS-20s, NATO's tactical nuclear weapons, those of the independent-minded French?

Reunification has at last given Germans the pleasure of living within stable borders as one country. Ever since the late nineteenth century, when Otto von Bismarck made a cohesive unit out of a fragmented collection of German states and principalities, Germany's condition has ranged from fair to horrible. Kaiser Wilhelm and Adolf Hitler led Germany into two devastating world wars. Even the past forty years of economic prosperity have been tempered by the realization that Germany was still the odds-on favorite as the primary battlefield in a third such war—if it were to come.

Instead, the collapse of the Soviet bloc—helped along in no small part by West Germany's economic success and stability—has opened the door for Germany's economic and cultural influence to spread more than ever across Europe and beyond. But forget the media scare that Germany is out to dominate, or that Germany will turn its back on the West in order to reap all the benefits of a newly democratized East. The reality is more complex. At the same time as Germany is spreading its influence, peacefully and democratically, the country also finds itself increasingly diluted into a larger European community.

Even before the reunification bomb was dropped on Germany, a great deal of noise was being made on the western front. The widely hyped 1992 initiative by the twelve members of the European Community to create the world's largest single market had already captured global attention. Given the enormity of the task, which involves harmonizing hundreds of invisible trade barriers from value-added taxes to the color of automobile headlights, only the most committed Euro-optimist could believe that on January 1, 1993, Europe's single market would be as efficient as that of the United States. Nevertheless, such healthy skepticism is a major step forward from the Euro-pessimism of the mid-1970s and early 1980s.

In fact, the EC's main problem now is to avoid being a victim of its own success. The list of candidates for admission is getting longer. Several could join without causing much disruption—Norway, Sweden, Switzerland, Austria. But Turkey? What about the Eastern Europe countries such as Poland, Hungary, Bulgaria, Romania and Czechoslovakia? These countries first have to convert to a market economy, but soon they too will be knocking on the EC's door.

Germans are understandably reluctant to jeopardize forty years of hard work and frugal savings only to be dragged down to the level of the lowest common economic denominator. Already Germany does not always get its way in the sticky negotiations to establish rules and directives for the existing EC members. The vaunted technical standards that reflect the excellence of German industry, for example, are being eroded. Common accounting rules will be more stringent than the current German rules, which allow companies to stash away hidden reserves for more than a few rainy days. On the most sensitive issue, the creation of a European central bank, Germans feel they have more to lose than to gain, since their deutsche mark is already the EC's de facto common currency.

Nobody knows exactly what Europe will look like in five or

ten years. The road to European unification has taken some
strange twists and turns since Robert Schuman proposed the
ground-breaking Coal and Steel Community in 1950. The six
original countries—France, Germany, Italy and the Benelux three
—have grown to twelve, all with increasingly disparate economies. Talk now is of a multispeed Europe, where the strongest
countries push economic and monetary integration further than
the weaker ones. Whatever happens, you can count on Germany
to be at the center of the storm.

Business the German Way

"Germany is at a crossroads. . . . Germany is going to be the
leading economic power in Europe. . . . Europe will be the largest single market in the world." Such notions are currently in
vogue, but they are almost always framed in the macroeconomic
terms described above. Just what role Germany will play in Europe and the world has aroused a great deal of interest, and magazines and books on the subject are proliferating. Nations,
however, do not produce prosperity; people and businesses do.
Up until now, there have been few attempts to provide outsiders
a glimpse of what goes on inside German business. For whatever
reason, observers in America and Europe have been blinded by
the rising sun of Japanese business, even though the culture that
underpins Japan is in many ways so alien as to be impossible to
adapt to Western business practices. Yet the analysis of Japan and
comparisons with America go on, generating a virtual industry of
books on both subjects. It is high time to take a closer look at
what has made Germany so successful.

The German way of doing business is clearly distinguishable
from the Japanese and American ways and, in light of Germany's
importance at the heart of an increasingly powerful Europe, merits a closer look. The idea of different models of capitalism is not
new. In December 1991 *International Herald Tribune* columnist
William Pfaff joined the debate of the capitalisms, a debate that is
sure to grow more heated in the decade of the 1990s. In Pfaff's
words, "America's is only one of several contemporary models of
capitalism, and on current evidence it is the least successful one."
Pfaff denounced the "pauperization" of U.S. workers through the

exploitation of unchecked free markets, especially since this pauperization has coincided with a spate of stunningly rich rewards
offered corporate leaders and financial types. For Pfaff, this pauperization is directly tied in with the reduced demand and recession that plagued the U.S. economy in 1991. The German model,
which Pfaff defined as "social consensus through worker participation, collective bargaining and social protection," is something
Pfaff believes the United States had better start considering more
seriously.

Several authors of books published recently have made much
the same argument, among them American authors Robert Kuttner and Daniel Burstein and French author and businessman
Michel Albert. The choice typically comes down to the three
primary capitalist models—Japanese, American, German-Euro-
pean—and the last one comes out looking pretty good. The Japanese model appears to be too culture-specific: neither Americans
nor Europeans are prepared to sacrifice so much of their individual
freedom for the greater glory of the corporation. The American
model, the zealous championing of free markets, has not prevented the continuing erosion of America's economic strength
relative to the rest of the world. Germany, meanwhile, continues
to grow in economic power, much like Japan, yet the German
social market model seems much more readily adaptable to other
Western countries. Germany's neighbors already look to Germany as a role model; perhaps the United States should, too.

The German way has many strengths indeed. The sense of
social concern for employees and the high value placed on jobs is
the human face that American capitalism all too often seems to
lack. But those gazing enviously at the greener grass on the other
side of the German fence should remember that the Germans are
themselves looking at methods of improving their way of doing
business. The great question for Germans is how to inject more
laissez-faire capitalism into their often rigid economy while pre-
serving the advantages of the social market economy.

The term "social market" is often bandied about when discussing German business, but a precise definition is hard to come
by. In fact, the social market is not so much a system as an ethic
developed after World War II. On May 10, 1945, the day after the
final armistice with the Allies was signed, Germans found rubble

piled everywhere. The Germans call this time the "zero hour," when the country started over from scratch. It was no time to argue about who should do what. Everybody who could work worked, and they helped those who could not. This kind of sentiment carried over to the marketplace. To be sure, the German economic miracle was made possible by the 1948 currency reform and the liberalizing economic reforms of Economics Minister Ludwig Erhard. But just as important was the fact that the Germans never gave up their strong sense of social responsibility.

Werner Otto: A Man of the First Hour

To understand German business today, you must come to terms with what the Germans went through during and immediately after the war. No one typifies the "men of the first hour," the entrepreneurs who started out amidst the rubble, better than Werner Otto. The themes that emerge from Otto's story—pragmatism, optimism, hard work, discretion and a strong sense of social responsibility—will reappear again and again throughout this book.

In 1949 Otto founded the Hamburg-based mail-order house Otto Versand; today, under the direction of his eldest son, Michael, the privately held company is the world's leading catalog company—at DM 20 billion in sales, ahead of Sears' catalog business as well as that of German rival Quelle. The Ottos own the Spiegel catalog in the United States, Otto Sumisho in Japan, 3 Suisses in France and Grattan in Britain.

Less widely known but also considerable is Otto's real estate business, built up through proceeds earned when he sold off stakes in Otto Versand to private investors in the early 1960s. In Germany, his ECE Group is the leading manager of shopping centers, with thirty-two already established and ten more under way in the old East Germany. In Toronto his Sagitta Group is active mostly in apartment and office buildings, while the New York–based Paramount Group oversees investments in office buildings and shopping centers everywhere from Manhattan to the suburbs of Chicago to Tulsa, Oklahoma.

At eighty-one, Werner Otto stays physically and mentally fit. He takes frequent walks in the country when he is not keeping an eye on business. His demeanor is enthusiastic and warm, but like many a successful—that is, wealthy—German, he prefers to keep a low profile. His experiences before, during and after the war have given him that mixture of caution and optimism that is so characteristic of Germans of his generation. While he has already described much of his entrepreneurial life with great lucidity in *Die Otto Gruppe,* published in 1983 but never translated from the German, he remains anxious not to appear in any magazine article. He did, however, agree to talk about his past and the current state of Germany for this book.

Werner Otto arrived in West Germany after the war as a refugee fleeing from the Russians with only a few marks in his pocket and the memory of a country gone berserk under Hitler. Before the war, Otto had spent most of his life in Prenzlau, outside Berlin, where his father ran a small wholesale food business. The business went bankrupt in the 1930s, when Otto was still a student. He was in his early twenties when Hitler came to power in 1933. As he describes it, he was politically aware, always debating world events with his friends and bewildered by the German people's inability to see what Hitler was doing. "We saw and thought Hitler would start the war. The people did not want to believe it. 'You see the tanks. Hitler is clearly rearming,' we would say. 'Oh, no,' the people would answer. They could not imagine what was happening. The propaganda was so strong. It was unbelievable."

Before the war, Otto was active in a conservative group that opposed the Nazis, and spent several years in jail. When the war broke out, he had to scramble to enlist in the regular army: his past made him a strong candidate for one of the 555 units. Says Otto, "These units were always given the most difficult assignments. They were cannon fodder." The Nazis assigned the 555 units, whose ranks consisted of undesirables, to such enviable tasks as sweeping mines from a field while under enemy fire. As a regular enlisted man, Otto survived the war, spending the last several months in an army hospital after suffering a head injury.

When the war ended on May 8, 1945, Werner Otto knew he did not want to stay in eastern Germany, which the Russian forces were expected to occupy shortly. He had a brother in Hamburg, so he headed there. Did he not fear the American occupying army? "Not at all," says Otto. "We hoped they would overrun the country first. We even said to ourselves, 'If only the people fighting on the western front would do a little less.' But in the war it was strange. As a young man you are full of ideas, and you discuss them with others your age and say, 'In my head I am against [the Nazis and the war],' but in the army you are so disciplined."

Thus, circumstances put Otto into Hamburg, then part of the British-occupied zone. He knew nothing about shoes, but there were a lot of barefoot people, so he started a shoe factory. His ignorance had one advantage, he later recalled: his optimism was not dampened by any professional knowledge. Thus he tackled seemingly impossible problems one at a time, much the way Germans removed pieces of rubble from their bombed-out cities one at a time.

Otto had no trouble finding people to work with: he put up an announcement that said, "Here something new is being started," and picked a few from the crowd that showed up. Wood to make the soles was readily available, leather a bit less so. The biggest problem was finding machines to sew the leather together and then onto the sole.

Using word of mouth—the Yellow Pages of the day—Otto tracked down a used-machine dealer who had set up shop amid a pile of rubble. Someone had brought the dealer the kind of machines Otto wanted after digging them out of a collapsed building to sell them as scrap iron. Instead, the dealer had put them into working order. Once he had the machines, Otto still had to procure heavy-duty thread. Since none was being produced, Otto improvised with a type of string used by farmers to bundle grain. The string was too rough to pass cleanly through the needles, so after every twenty stitches or so, the sewer had to stop and rethread the needle. The work was tiring, and a sewer was lucky to finish twenty pairs of shoes in a day. But, as Otto says, "none of that bothered us. We went forward, we produced."

Then the currency reform of 1948 opened up trade between the various occupied zones, and Otto's shoe company was suddenly no match for the high-quality shoemakers from the Rhineland in the French zone. He had to start over again. He sold off most of his inventory, paid his bills and found he had DM 6,000 in his pocket, a production site, some outmoded machinery and a new car that would serve him in his next venture.

In his book, Werner Otto wrote that he never suspected that starting Otto Versand would be the path to great business success. It was more a question of "What can I do now?" Shoe production was out, and entering the retail market struck him as too difficult. He recalled having seen a mail-order catalog several years earlier and figured he'd create one for shoes. He rounded up some of his last inventory and went shopping in the same Rhineland shoe factories that had put him out of business. He had twenty-eight different kinds of shoes photographed. Then he and his coworkers glued the photos by hand into some 300 catalogs and wrote in the prices underneath.

The rest, to use a cliché, is history. The Otto Group grew rapidly during the 1950s and 1960s, boom years in Germany, and then expanded abroad beginning in the 1970s. Today the company distributes over 300 million catalogs in thirteen countries.

Having experienced the postwar reconstruction of West Germany firsthand, Werner Otto speaks with authority on the challenges of rebuilding the newly reunified East. The revolutionary changes that began with the toppling of the Berlin Wall in November 1989 caught Otto—like so many others—by surprise. Originally from the East and a nationalist by temperament, Otto had nevertheless given up almost all hope on the region. But he had not given up on the people there. In the concluding chapter of his 1983 book on the Otto Group, Otto wrote, "I am convinced that entrepreneurs above all share responsibility in supporting the well-being of our society. Without the initiatives of entrepreneurs and the efforts of the workers the reconstruction after the war would not have been possible. The workers in East Germany are no worse than ours in the West—the economic leadership in the East has failed because of the government bureaucrats."

And now that German reunification has opened the door to entrepreneurship in the East, many observers equate the situation there with the one that existed after the war in West Germany. Otto points out, however, that the two situations are by no means identical.

Shortly after East Germany was opened for travel, he made a trip by car through the recouped lands. As Otto describes the trip, his usually pragmatic tone and demeanor shifts slightly, becoming almost wistful. "I drove through the countryside. There were so few cars, the streets were the same as before. From the outside you could not always see how bad the houses really are. For me, it was actually just like the old days . . . it was magical. In my youth the houses were also not all painted either. There was a fair amount of poverty. No one had the money to do anything. The façades didn't look that much better than today."

But soon the pragmatist resurfaces: "Naturally, all the fixtures worked back then and the stairs to the buildings were in good shape."

How long does Otto think it will take to get the fixtures working in East Germany? "Not just the politicians painted a rosy picture, but many economic forecasters too. I believe the trend will be down until 1993, and then the economy will start to pick up. It took us twenty years to turn West Germany around."

Otto sees big differences between the first economic miracle and the prospects of a second. "We had rubble, nothing at hand, we had to help ourselves. It was at zero. Even the competition started out at zero. We were inspired; we had to improvise; each year we tried to optimize. Every step was a step forward. We were always positive, believing in the future. We had just had this horrible experience with Hitler, and we had the feeling: 'We survived, we can start over.'

"How it is now?" he asks rhetorically. "I called old cousins of mine who live in the East and said, 'Ah, it's difficult, you have nothing there.' They answered, 'What do you mean, nothing here? We have these factories.' They could not understand that overnight their factories had become worthless. The plants are no longer capable of producing, but the people have yet to understand this. Also, the competition from the West appears to them to be overpowerful. The East Germans see a huge mountain they have to climb. How do they get out of where they are? It's a terrible feeling, a huge psychological uncertainty. This uncertainty is the biggest obstacle that must be overcome. I would say that it is an enormous psychological and political process. It is economic, of course, as well, but the spiritual burden, the sense of hopelessness, is immense.

"I am also worried about possible political problems," continues Otto. "There is a danger that the old socialist tendency makes a comeback and capitalism goes. We can't forget that the old elements are still there and will try to make use of the psychological hopelessness to further their cause. The economic need there is not so dramatic since people have the safety net. But the uncertainty . . . bit steps are needed.

"Then there are practical problems. When I started out after the war, there was a demand for everything. I started the shoe company without knowing anything about shoes, and the shoes we made weren't anything special, but everybody was happy to get them. Then the French zone opened up, and I had to close the company. But the first steps had been taken. I had a fairly big plant, and I had saved DM 6,000. I started the mail-order house. We could live and get by with small steps. But now in what was East Germany, they need big steps. And how do you convince people that in five years they will be okay, but that for the next three they will have large-scale unemployment?"

Otto also knows the importance of putting certain issues to rest. He has no sympathy for the far-right German conservatives who insist on the return of the eastern German lands seized by Poland after the war—and officially conceded by Germany in a treaty with Poland on June 17, 1991. Says Otto, "You hear the speeches and the rhetoric, but it does not really reach [most Germans]. That is clear. We started the war, we were wrong. There has to be an end."

On a touchier subject, what to do with the old collaborators of the East German regime, Otto recalls his experience right after the war: "At the beginning it was a shock to me, because I was a politically thinking person, that the people did not cry out [about the Nazis or those who helped them]. But I would say it was quickly over. Perhaps too many people felt themselves guilty. Then there was the question of what to do with the people in the party. I had friends who were in the Nazi party. They were against the war every bit as much as I was. They imagined something completely different when they joined. But they couldn't do anything. If they tried to quit the party, they would end up in a concentration camp. The distinction between being in the party or not was very muddled.

"Now, in the old East Germany, there are two sorts. I spoke with a young man two years ago who wanted to study, and I asked if he would join the Communist party. 'No,' he said; he did not want anything to do with the party. If I were a young man, I would not have joined the party either. Today, I am older and more laid back. A lot of people saw that to get anywhere you had to join the party. They might have been more against what was going on than people who were not in the party. There are guilty people who should be punished, but for the bulk of the people we have to draw an end. It's a new beginning."

Otto puts his faith in a new beginning for Germany, not the sort of change that might fundamentally disrupt the themes that have made western Germany so strong: "I hope we soon create conditions in the East like those in the West and that we don't have any major political changes. Some parties lean toward socialism because they cannot understand a capitalist or free market system."

Indeed, with whole industries like steel and chemicals going down in the East, many East Germans must be wondering if capitalism isn't in fact as ghastly and coldhearted as the old communist propaganda suggested. Given the shock treatment to which East Germany is being subjected, some doubt is understandable. The irony is that West Germans pride themselves on their social concern within a capitalist framework.

Consider Otto's comments on the social responsibility of his company toward employees: "I feel this is one of the most important foundations of our company. We are not an anonymous company, we are a team, or a community. One must think that employees *are* the company. For example, we established an emergency fund for our workers. This kind of thing was common in the first reconstruction years after the war, when everyone started out small. It instilled a feeling of togetherness, and came not from the government but from the common need of the times."

As Otto indicates, the German social market economy is not just the government taking out a bigger percentage of a worker's pay in order to provide health care and meet other social needs. It is a business ethic. Otto mentioned in his book how the company's emergency fund had been used several years earlier to buy the freedom of an employee held by the East German police after she had been involved in an auto accident there. For this action, Otto never made the headlines as did the American entrepreneur H. Ross Perot, who had his employees jetted out of Teheran by a SWAT team in the early days of the Iranian revolution. But Otto's employee was no less happy.

Otto Versand's social commitment is not just financial. Otto created a special bureau to handle personal problems his employees might have in relation to their work or outside. Otto credits this bureau for having maintained the sense of togetherness from the early days, even after the firm had grown into a large corporation. Otto gave his onetime secretary Gisela Marcus control over the bureau; as he wrote in his book, "She knew well that she could expect all my help." Otto's philosophy toward employees and people in general is summed up nicely in his book: "One must be open and speak to the positive side in people."

Otto also offers a fairly unusual—by American standards—appraisal of unions, which enabled a steady progression in the standard of living. Without the unions, writes Otto, progressive entrepreneurs who wanted to pay higher wages to their workers would have been uncompetitive against entrepreneurs who adopted a low-wage policy. His only complaint is the unions' tendency to want to get involved in companies' management decision-making process.

Of course, Otto did not build a large corporation by being a pushover. He recounted in his book how much trouble he had early on finding the right advertising manager. Creative advertising was virtually nonexistent in Germany after so many years of Josef Goebbels and Nazi propaganda. Within the first seven years of his company's founding, Otto tried twelve different people in the advertising post, only to let them go. The other employees were betting on how many months the thirteenth would last, but they probably all lost: Wolfgang Thill kept the post for twenty years, until his retirement.

Often, German entrepreneurs and managers will say they would like more freedom to hire and fire, as their counterparts in

America do, but Otto does not see Germany as being at a disadvantage in this respect. "The hire and fire has an advantage and a disadvantage. The advantage is you can get rid of someone quickly. The disadvantage is that the good man leaves much more quickly when he has another opportunity. It's not that we try to keep our employees [from leaving], but that they don't leave our company so much because they have more loyalty to the company."

The notion that a company is part of the social fabric of a community is well developed in Germany. In a few cases, German businessmen have relocated their company's headquarters to Switzerland in order to save on taxes. Such a move strikes many German entrepreneurs as treachery, but Werner Otto is a bit more sanguine: "I was speaking with people in my company in the early 1960s who told me, 'Herr Otto, we should move our headquarters to Switzerland because we could save a lot in taxes.' I thought about it, and then came back and said, 'I don't want to hear about this subject anymore. I pay my taxes in Germany, in the country where my employees went to school, where my clients live.' "

Otto continues, "In the old days we called this *preußische Haltung* [the virtuous side of Prussian behavior], but I would be careful not to call it that now for the interpretations it might raise. I understand the people who did [move], though. Not all. There are unscrupulous people who do things only for money. As an entrepreneur, one has a responsibility. Money is not everything."

Otto's apparent willingness to pay corporate taxes in Germany, where for many years the rate was a hefty 56 percent (it has since come down slightly), might seem excessively benevolent to tightfisted entrepreneurs abroad. But the other side of the coin is the small German tax base. Otto grins and sums it up in a phrase: "In Germany one does not show profits gladly." He admits that the German system of financial disclosure—where assets are written down quickly and hidden reserves abound—needs to be changed, and he embraces efforts under way in the European Community to harmonize balance sheet and income statement reporting. "But," adds Otto with a knowing smile, "even with a new accounting system, [our businesses] won't necessarily show any more profit."

Just as discretion in showing profits is ever present at the German corporation, so too with the entrepreneur. Otto, for example, is comfortable using a nondescript house in a nondescript neighborhood for an office. He could easily afford his own jet, but he chooses to fly with the regular commercial airlines (although he says he occasionally charters a Lear jet when necessary). "Perhaps we lived through so much—World War I, the Depression, inflation, World War II—that we have no respect for ostentation."

Nor does Otto deliberately seek favor in the press for his charity. He established one of Germany's first clinics for handicapped children outside of Hamburg, but he declines to discuss his role there in great detail. "The work is more important than talking about it." He knows too that Germans are quick to scoff at anything that smacks of self-aggrandizing public relations.

Perhaps that is one reason Otto—like many other wealthy Germans and Europeans—is less inhibited in the United States. His recent donation to the museum of Harvard University, which is building the Werner Otto Hall, devoted to twentieth-century art, is the type of glamour giving he has shunned back home. Says Otto, "I wanted to give back something to the country that gave Germany so much." Of course, Harvard is a good address.

Quoting the popular ad campaign, Otto also says he loves New York. He likes the city that never sleeps for the same reasons most people do: the twenty-four-hour hustle and bustle, the cultural diversity, the anonymity, the arts and so on. But he admits to having been shocked by the poverty when he first arrived there in 1954. "How can such a rich country have such poverty? That would be impossible in Germany." But now, says Otto, "I've gotten used to it." Still, he fully understands how someone who rides the subway to work every day might not. He adds, "New York is a place where much poverty is concentrated, and the [federal] government has to do its part. The New Yorker cannot do it alone." Even for a German free-market capitalist like Otto, the notion that the federal government should do more comes naturally.

The sense of social responsibility is not the only area that sets German companies apart. Otto describes his initial experience of visiting various mail-order houses in the United States in the 1950s: "I was amazed at how antiquated the American companies were, with simple production lines and very labor-intensive methods. I was surprised. What strikes me in America is that unlike Germans, who constantly optimize a company with small improvements, Americans prefer to wait and build something completely new. Americans don't have the high-quality middle management that we have. There is no one on the operational level who can make those slight modifications and improvements. Everything is directed from above, or specialists are brought in, and then something is built up from scratch."

The lack of quality middle management in America is a point Otto repeats several times in the conversation. "It's unfathomable to [Germans] how America can function," says Otto, more bewildered than critical. What the United States lacks, in Otto's view, is anything like the German apprenticeship system, where young employees spend a few years in company training programs. "Also, it's hard in America because if you train somebody, he takes that skill and goes elsewhere, whereas in Germany people figure, this company trained me, so I'll stay here."

Yet Otto has many positive things to say about the United States. He talks about the willingness at Spiegel to adopt new management techniques and learn new ways. "The Americans are not at all like the Europeans, who are more stuck in their ways. When we bought the 3 Suisses catalog in France, we had to bring in younger managers who would adopt our methods." Spiegel management, on the other hand, readily adopted exacting specifications on how dress manufacturers must pack their dresses, what size hangers to use and so on.

Nor does he think Germans necessarily work harder than Americans or anybody else. If anything, "Germans work more intensively," says Otto. "They don't regard hard work as just a job, but as a task or duty."

The talk of work as a duty raises the comparison to the Japanese work ethic. He likes Japan, having visited there as early as 1964. Especially fascinating, he finds, is the Japanese work force's *Zusammengehörigkeitsgefühl,* their feeling of belonging together. But he laughs a little as he acknowledges that some of the practices, like the early-morning calisthenics, seem perhaps a bit militaristic. And would Otto think of using Japanese methods in

Germany? Before the question is finished, Otto is laughing harder and shaking his head: "No."

As our conversation winds down, the subject turns to the pros and cons of mail order versus retail shopping. Otto describes a recent experience: "You know, I was having trouble finding a pair of shoes I could wear because I have sensitive feet. One person from Otto Versand said to me, 'Why don't you try a pair out of the catalog? They're very comfortable.' So I tried a pair from my own company, and sure enough, they were comfortable. Of course, it's not that surprising. In a normal shoe store, a shoe that does not please the customer simply goes back on the rack. But the mail-order house loses a sale and incurs shipping costs every time a shoe is sent back, so the incentive to carry only the products that will sell is greater."

Werner Otto's anecdote about the right pair of shoes is an excellent reminder that success in business does not depend on national traits, government programs, sophisticated management techniques, innovative financing and the like. Success comes down to making and selling a product that people want to buy and having the common sense to know it when you've got it. The rest is secondary.

PART ONE

THE BUSINESS OF
GERMAN BUSINESS

"The head of a Mittelstand company has, and rightly so, the same sense of self-worth as the head of Daimler Benz."

—GÜNTER KAYSER

2

Let There Be Order: The Style and Substance of German Management

Werner Otto's story—like so many others involving the early days of the postwar German economic miracle—has taken on a mythical quality in contemporary Germany. Few Germans nowadays can conceive of the degree of improvisation necessary to survive and rebuild amid the postwar chaos and rubble. Today, German business thrives not on chaos but on order. Everything about German business, from the German style of management within the corporation to the general environment in which the corporation operates, is heavily structured—a point of frustration for many outsiders. Perhaps it's genetic, a Germanic predisposition to orderliness. Or perhaps it's Germany's turbulent history, which understandably instills a heavy fear of risk. Whatever the reason, if something moves, trust the Germans to try to nail it down.

The Stereotype

Take the typically Germanic chemicals industry. Dr. Wolfgang Brühl, chief economist at Frankfurt-based Hoechst AG, one of Germany's big three chemical concerns along with BASF and Bayer, knows the business well: "In the chemicals industry, the corporate structure has a functional and scientific quality. We see the company as a construction where certain things run together, more than as an organic entity." In other words, the organization of the various divisions and subsidiaries is very rationalized, with a clear hierarchy. As for management, rank may not be quite as pronounced as in the army, but it's close.

Or IBM in Germany. John Hormann, a German native, is a longtime IBM manager who lived and worked for much of his life in the United States before returning to work in Germany. He indirectly confirms Brühl's point, but with a decidedly negative spin. If you think IBM in America is a paragon of rationality in corporate business, says Hormann, it's nothing compared to IBM in Germany. "In America I had thirty-six engineers working for me and I never saw the hierarchy: first line, second line, third line or anything. If I told people, 'We have to come up with a way to get such and such done,' the Americans would take the ball and run with it. In Germany, I had twenty-five engineers at the plant in Sindelfingen. Their attitude was, 'You tell us what you want us to do.' It's the attitude we called *Obrigkeit*."

Typically, German management does not inspire results through easygoing interaction and Friday beer bashes, but because Germans attack work with determination. John Hormann points to German work habits as one reason German managers actually take their six weeks of vacation: "They need them. After they're at work, battling to get projects done within a certain deadline, they have to flee the workplace."

Another case: Pierre Pierremont comfortably managed a Brit-ish-owned paint company in France for years before the company was sold to a Hoechst subsidiary in 1982. Suddenly life at work changed. Company meetings became more formalized as Pierremont was expected to file extensive reports to the parent company on what took place, who said what, and what decisions, if any, were agreed upon. At one point, an exasperated Pierremont asked his superiors if they wanted him to produce paint or reports on paint. Eventually the Germans mellowed: now Pierremont lists only the names of a meeting's participants and the final outcome.

The method in this German management madness is to achieve a higher state of *Zusammenarbeit,* or "working together." In fact, all the formalized consensus seeking, intended to eliminate strife, also allows managers to cover their "arsches." Whether it leads to better management can be debated.

One Englishman who has spent many years in the insurance business, traveling widely and dealing at the most senior level with Germans and other nationals, also found that working with Germans could be irritating. As he put it: "I try to put aside that I was a schoolboy in London when they came over and dropped bombs . . . but the average German has an innate arrogance. Yet, coupled with that arrogance, he has a readiness to be servile. I used to watch people in Germany and was struck by the manner in which they spoke with subordinates, or the way they changed when a superior came into the room.

"There is also a tremendous lack of humor. When they are sitting in a beer garden and the music goes dum-dum-dum, they can laugh. But in a room, when something bad happens, no one can come up with a joke.

"Nor are the Germans very good at adapting to changed circumstances. They try to beat things to conform to the plan. Dealing with uncertainty *is* the insurance business. To believe you can write a script is incredibly naive, yet that is what they do."

Naturally, anecdotes about working with the Germans can vary depending on the speaker. Fortunately, there is a lighter side to the Germans than the one described above. Florence Gérard, who spent several years working for a German consulting firm, jotted down some tips in an alumni newsletter for any of her French compatriots who might have to work with their neighbors across the Rhine. An excerpt:

If you work for a German company, especially in Germany, you will notice the importance of customs, norms and procedures as well as the systematic organization of everything, even down to those activities normally known for their creativity.

These simple practical tips should help you adapt to the daily life of a German company.

Of all the customs to respect, the use of titles is primary. Your financial officer, having completed his doctorate, will forever be Dr. Schmidt; in fact, it's written on his official identity card. Even after ten years spent in an office facing his, you will still call him Dr. Schmidt.

The respect for titles is accompanied by a respect for diplomas and degrees no matter what the level. An engineer would not be faithful to himself if he did not add "Dipl. Ing." after his name on his card.

Do not interrupt the person with whom you are speaking even if you have figured out what he is about to say. Let the person get there by himself; otherwise he may be disoriented for the rest of the conversation because you have broken the coherence and continuity of his speech.

Manage your time like a precious commodity: never be late for meetings, get to the point, don't leave a visitor waiting, and don't disrupt the planning of a group unless there's an act of God. There's no point in staying at the office until 8:00 at night—either no one will be there to notice, or they will just think that you are poorly organized.

Depending on your temperament, you may find the German style of organization either creatively stifling or an efficient way to help you concentrate on your job. Anyway, your personal work habits will be transformed, and you will even find yourself being surprised at the lack of rigor and the waste of energy that can be observed in other countries.

The Reality

One thing is clear: if German business is successful, it is not thanks to some secret, previously unheralded management method. Authors touting the latest in fabulous Japanese or American or Tibetan management styles have little to fear from the Germans. But then again, not all German companies fit the rigid management stereotype. As we shall see, the Mittelstand, the medium-size German companies, are on the whole much more important to German business than the large corporations, and these smaller companies—and their widely varying management styles—are heavily influenced by their owners. And plenty of large German companies maintain unique ownership structures that allow for much more flexible management.

In the last decade, Peter Harf, now in his mid-forties, has turned the old-line chemicals firm Joh. A. Benckiser GmbH from a medium-size producer of basic commodity chemicals such as citric acid into a highly profitable consumer brands company. With the rapid acquisition of detergent manufacturers (Panigal, Camp, Mira Lanza) and cosmetic companies (Lancaster, Margaret Astor), sales went from DM 450 million in 1980 before Harf arrived to over DM 3.2 billion in 1990—and interest on the debt is more than covered by operating cash flow. Harf, whose Rhineland accent gives away his Cologne origins, received an M.B.A. from Harvard, then worked for several years for the Boston Consulting Group in Germany. He was nevertheless lured to Benckiser because, as he says, "the management structure makes it very attractive to work here."

As CEO, Harf enjoys substantial independence from Benckiser's owners as well as all the advantages of a private company. Benckiser's share capital is divided evenly among eleven members of the Reimann family, whose ancestor, Johann A. Benckiser, founded the company in 1823. Albert Reimann, who retired in 1975 as the last family member to serve as chief executive, gave his trusted adviser and successor, Martin Gruber, the voting power for 60 percent of the company shares. Gruber was chief executive for a few years but selected Harf to take over the company management while he continued to represent the family interests. Says Harf, "The Reimann family still owns the shares, but as long as I've got Mr. Gruber on my side, we can act like owners. That's the whole trick. There are no minority shareholders, no banks on the board, no complicated discussion on what our projects are."

Harf sums up the Reimann family's situation: "They have given up operating control, and it would even be hard for them to divest. That obviously takes a big leap of faith. We have a

contract now, and things are settled. In twenty years we will
probably have to find a solution with someone from the family
for another twenty-five years."

Harf has used his independence to flatten company management and kill off the sacred cows. "When I got here, we had an
old, unprofitable, highly bureaucratized parent and [politically]
weak foreign subsidiaries. They were successful mainly against
the directives of the parent. Here they played big games, big
company, and the guys on the outside were making the money.
Our first job was to run the non-German businesses.

"Before, the company was fully integrated, like a typical
German company. The management here was both functionally
responsible for the parent and had directive competence internationally. As a result, they were completely preoccupied in coordinating German operations, constantly fighting. They would
be here from 6 A.M. until 8 P.M. discussing piddly stuff about
German operations.

"Today, we have no organigrams, no procedure book. We
did have some in the past. Two or three of my colleagues early
on here took six months writing fifty pages on how to apply for,
make, control and manage investments in a consumer products
company—it's a joke. Our annual investment budget is about 2
percent of sales. You sign on a piece of paper what marketing can
spend, and then the managers have to agonize over a ten-page
document to make sure they conform. We got rid of that.

"Half our project list never happens. But all that stuff I tell
Mr. Gruber. We discuss it, he gives me feedback very easily. With
time you know when he gets extremely nervous and upset. We
just constantly discuss things. It's like two pieces of a puzzle. Put
the two of us together, and you've got the independent family
entrepreneur who runs his own company and does what he
wants. The moment we are not in agreement, he clearly has the
stronger cards. As in the United States, ownership still gives you
the ultimate control."

While the Benckiser ownership structure is slightly unusual, it
is by no means unique. Quite a few German family-owned companies are structured in similar fashion, where the families have
little control over management.

Legally Speaking

The highly structured, formalized life within many German firms makes itself very visible in the larger German business environment. Take the laws governing German business, for example. They are all codified, and few areas of German business life are unaffected: commercial law, civil law, corporate law, labor law, and countless other codes tell businessmen what they can and cannot do. If something is not written in a code, or if the situation seems gray, Germans think twice—and then sit tight. One area in which the German legal codes are particularly vague: the laws governing so-called hostile corporate takeovers. Not surprisingly, hostile takeovers in Germany have been virtually nonexistent (other reasons are discussed in Chapter Five).

The common-law system in the United States, where one might say that everything not expressly forbidden is allowed, provides far more room for wheeling and dealing. But most German businessmen gladly give up that freedom in return for certainty and the knowledge that a coterie of lawyers is not persistently trailing them around. Peter Harf says what all too many U.S. businessmen already know: "Lawyers in the United States have an extremely powerful position. They take advantage, both in terms of their fees and in trying to tell businesspeople how to run their shop. Here, the way you structure a transaction, you don't have to write everything into a contract." Of course no American businessman with half an ego would say that the lawyers run his shop, but then little business gets done in the United States without lawyers, and at a cost.

The advantages of an explicit legal code have not been altogether lost on U.S. businessmen, and in some areas the United States has drawn closer to European codified law. The Uniform Commercial Code, for example, which spells out the rights of buyers and sellers, has been adopted into law by a good majority of state legislatures. But the United States has a long way to go in reducing the influence of lawyers.

More worrisome for German business is the creeping influence of the American legal system in Germany. More and more American law firms have opened offices in Germany, spreading the

American style of law practice. German law firms naturally like the style, but businessmen complain about the ever-thickening contracts and their numbing redundancy.

The German penchant for organization goes beyond the legal system, affecting the very essence of German capitalism. All this organization appears not so much in the form of a centralized industrial policy or in vast and powerful cartels and oligopolies. True, the German government has subsidized some hard-hit industries like coal and shipbuilding and has helped build up the aerospace industry. But to say that the German economy is guided by government ministers would be off the mark. Similarly, competition in most German industries is fierce, even if some display oligopolistic tendencies. Thus three of Germany's largest utilities had no trouble getting together when the East German government was collapsing in early 1990 and agreeing to take over the production of power.

Don't Rock the Boat

The orderliness of German capitalism has more to do with a basic philosophy that abhors rocking the boat. When Americans think of not rocking the boat, they think of leaving the market to its own caprices. Companies may rise, companies may fall, but the market lives on. In Germany, not rocking the boat means taking the sting out of the market and to some extent protecting the status quo.

Nowhere is this attitude more evident than in the shareholding of large German corporations, especially the banks. With their numerous ownership stakes in German industrial companies, German banks have an unparalleled influence in the German economy. When a bank owns 25 percent of an industrial company and a banker heads that company's supervisory board, the company in question knows it has a steady line of credit through thick and thin.

German corporate shareholdings offer other advantages. Consider Allianz, Germany's (and Europe's) leading insurance company, which holds a 25 percent stake in the Münchener Rückversicherungs-Gesellschaft (Munich Re), Germany's—and the world's—largest reinsurer. Would Munich Re, which also happens to own 25 percent of Allianz, be the world's largest reinsurance company if the business from partially owned companies like Allianz were subtracted? (After all, Allianz has some incentive to give its reinsurance business to Munich Re, presumably reaping benefits in the form of dividends later.) Another reinsurer, competing worldwide with Munich Re, figured that if the business received from its partially owned clients were subtracted, Munich Re would be less powerful than it appears to be.

German companies seem to be forever buying stakes in other companies instead of investing in their own businesses. Not all the stakes are visible, since stakes below 25 percent need not be reported. On the whole, very few German public corporations have their stock widely distributed, since usually a bank or other industrial company owns a sizable chunk of stock. Take Philipp Holzmann AG, Germany's largest construction company. Some 30 percent of the company is owned by Deutsche Bank, while another 20 percent is owned by Germany's second largest construction company, Hochtief AG, which in turn is 25 percent owned by the Rheinisch-Westfälisches Elektrizitätswerk (RWE) utility. Over 5 percent of RWE's stock is rumored to be in the hands of the Werhahn family, which also owns a 50 percent stake in Germany's fourth largest construction company, Strabag Bau AG. Examples like this are common throughout German industry.

It would be handy to report that the various strings of German corporate ownership all lead back to a guy named Hans or Dieter, who would then explain the rationale behind all the crossholdings —but no such luck. Most of the time, the German stakes in other companies are minority stakes, just enough for some degree of influence but not enough to pose a demonstrable threat. Part of the problem is that, by law, German companies may only buy back limited amounts of their own stock. So, as a precaution against unfriendly takeovers, they find an ally to buy a strategic stake. But in collectively grabbing on to one another, German corporations are also in a sense overcoming their basic fear of the unknown. The overall capital in all the various companies may be reduced, and growth possibilities may be more limited as a result, but that's okay with the Germans. There are fewer potential disruptions that way.

The comparison between this German system of cross-ownership and the Japanese *keiretsu* system, where companies within a large group such as Mitsubishi own stakes in one another, is not altogether inaccurate. The differences, however, are important. The noticeably more cohesive Japanese groups work together for the common enrichment of the group. It's easy to identify the companies forming the Mitsubishi group: Mitsubishi Bank, Mitsubishi Heavy Industries, Mitsubishi Motor, Mitsubishi Electric, Mitsubishi Chemical and another twenty or so. To sell their stakes in one another, thus destroying the group's cohesiveness, would be anathema.

Such clearly identifiable groups do not exist in Germany; consequently, there is no clear sense of a group purpose. Instead, the German system consists of a series of constantly shifting alliances. Blocks of shares occasionally change hands—although the German tax code, with a more than 50 percent tax on certain capital gains not reinvested, naturally makes companies reluctant to sell their stakes. Moreover, Germans are perfectly capable of letting pride and ego get in the way of the group purpose, much more so than in Japan.

If Germans do not like seeing the boat rocked, they positively hate seeing the boat sunk. Bankruptcy in Germany carries a heavy stigma. Only when the last creditor has been paid can a German entrepreneur who has gone bankrupt hope to get credit again. The famous collapse in 1974 of the Herstatt Bank because of illegal currency speculation caused the bank's majority owner, the late Hans Gerling (who was caught unaware by the illegal speculation), to sell 51 percent of his profitable insurance business just to raise DM 210 million and help pay back creditors. Compare that to the United States, where the former owner of a bankrupt savings and loan can walk away without paying as much as $210.

Trade Fairs and Trade Associations

The German legal system and the system of intertwined corporate stakes have perhaps the most far-reaching influence on German business, but there are other more benign—if telling—ways in which Germans like to organize business.

The *Messe,* or trade fair, is hardly peculiar to Germany, but the Germans are passionate about theirs. The fall trade fair in Frankfurt, which covers all sorts of consumer goods, has a 750-year history and bills itself as the oldest trade fair in the world. The larger fairs, like the Frankfurt book fair, draw businesses and customers from around the world, while others, like the camping and crafts fair, serve a very local clientele. But no German industry or trade goes without a fair, nor would German companies think of skipping the events. The press reports widely on all the goings-on, who came out with what product, what's hot, what's not, and so forth. Six cities—Frankfurt, Düsseldorf, Cologne, Munich, Hannover and Berlin—offer permanent facilities and attract the largest fairs, while the Leipzig fair, formerly a window to the East when Germany was divided, has now lost its attraction and is struggling to keep pace.

Industry and trade associations are also much more important in Germany than in the United States and other countries. Whereas in the United States, private lobbyists buttonhole politicians on behalf of wealthy corporations, German trade associations, with their democratically elected leaders, do the talking. One reason: Germans can be almost pathological in their quest for fairness, and they see the system of private lobbyists as favoring the deep-pocketed corporations over the little guys. Of course, lobbyists in Germany are not unknown: they just lobby the association leaders more than the politicians.

The largest of the umbrella groups are the Bundesverband der Deutschen Industrie and the Deutscher Industrie- und Handelstag, where top executives from all sorts of different companies confer on matters of general concern to German business. Most recently, the associations' executives consulted with government leaders over stronger export controls to prevent further embarrassments like the shipments of German-made chemical plants to Iraq and Libya. On a more regular basis, the associations' staffs put out statistics on the general state of business.

The power of these associations cannot be underestimated. Several local associations cover retail trade in Germany; together with the unions they've been particularly effective in maintaining Germany's ridiculous store-closing law—the *Ladenschlußgesetz*—against all reason. While many countries have blue laws limiting store hours, Germany's law is so restrictive that it's an embarrassment. All stores, from major department stores to supermarkets to mom-and-pop shops, have to close by 6:30 P.M. during the week, by noon on Saturday, and all day on Sunday. The associations and unions did make a concession not long ago when they allotted one Saturday per month for shopping until 6:30 P.M.

Strict enforcement of the law can lead to some farcical situations. One loophole allows stores in train stations, airports and gas stations to stay open later than usual during the week and on Sundays. The exception, thoughtfully provided to satisfy the needs of travelers, does not prevent nontravelers from picking up a tube of toothpaste at the train station on Sunday afternoon. But the retail trade associations, instead of looking to relax the store-closing law so that all stores can compete on an equal footing, have gone in the opposite direction. One Hamburg association petitioned the local court in 1991 to make the stores at the train station distinguish between real travelers and fake ones, and to distinguish between real travel needs and nonessential items. Thus the court handed down a ruling in early 1992 that would, in effect, say it's okay to buy handkerchiefs on Sunday, but not T-shirts. Apparently the culture that produced Immanuel Kant and Adolf Hitler still seems capable of turning its back on reason in the name of reason.

The Stamp of Quality

The store-closing law is one of those embarrassing examples of the German ability to take things to extremes; it's a kind of caricature. The good side of the German character, however, is thoroughness, which Germans more often than not put to good advantage. Take the excellent reputation for quality enjoyed by German products everywhere. As consumers, Germans have been raised to demand the highest quality; as manufacturers, they organize their businesses to satisfy that demand.

Robert Rademacher, who runs the largest distributorship for Volkswagen, Audi and Porsche in Germany, knows all about demanding German consumers. He explains that when it comes to cars, Germans want perfection. "In the United States, the average customer has a Ford or a GM and does not care if the car has a small dent. Here in Germany, as soon as there's the smallest scratch in the car fender, probably two thirds of the owners take the car to the body shop on their very next trip.

"We also have a very critical technical press here which looks at every small detail in the car that is not optimal. These articles are widely read by car buyers. That forces the manufacturers to spend a lot of money on small details, which may or may not be a good thing."

But then pointing down to the roof of the spare parts department of his company's headquarters outside of Düsseldorf, Rademacher reemphasizes the need for quality: "In the old days we dealt with about twenty thousand replacement engines. Today, only about four thousand. The manager of the spare parts department is sad about it, and the decrease hurts our earnings. But if we replaced so many engines per year, we'd lose our clients. That's why our argument here in Germany can only be more quality. We have to concentrate so that the customer comes in only once a year for a maintenance check. In the old days you got a gold watch when your Volkswagen made it over a hundred thousand kilometers [60,000 miles]. Today the cars can easily get four hundred thousand kilometers [250,000 miles]. Volkswagen would need to own a watch company."

On the manufacturing side, Germans have a long history of stressing quality. As we shall see, the tradition of skilled labor, which originated with the apprenticeship system of the Middle Ages, is still very much alive today. Moreover, for the better part of the last four centuries, beginning with the devastating effects of the Thirty Years' War, Germany has essentially been a seller's market. It's easy to forget that Germany was not always the wealthy country it is today. Goods in Germany were frequently scarce, so if a shoemaker got his hands on a rare piece of leather, he was inclined to make a shoe that would last and last.

Today, German business is still organized to privilege high-quality manufacturing. German accounting allows for very rapid depreciation, for example, which enables German manufacturers to keep buying the latest in machinery. German technical standards are far more exacting than those in other countries. And then there is the technical supervisory association, the Technischer Überwachungsverein, which the Germans call the TÜV (rhymes a bit with "roof").

Most Germans deal with the TÜV at least once a year, when they go to get their car inspected. The TÜVs are independent, nonprofit associations—each German state has one, but they are not part of the government, strictly speaking. Their creation goes back to the late 1800s, when the steam boilers commonly used for energy had a nasty habit of blowing up unpredictably and killing everyone in the vicinity. The German government of the day decided that these potential hazards needed to be inspected. From that point on, there was no stopping the TÜVs' expansion. It seemed that around every German corner lurked a danger and a German in need of protection.

The TÜVs took on the task of inspecting all potentially dangerous products. At first it was motorcars, elevators and electrical equipment; then came entire TÜV bureaus devoted to, say, nuclear technology or medical equipment. But with their classic thoroughness, the Germans realized that inspecting the machines alone just wasn't good enough. You had to inspect the humans too. Thus, in addition to qualified engineers, the TÜVs have a staff of psychiatrists. Say a German with a history of alcoholism goes to apply for a driver's license. If the driver's license bureau has doubts about the applicant, it can send him to the TÜV to get checked out. Only when he comes back stamped with a TÜV seal of approval does he get the license.

Getting the TÜV seal of approval is mandatory in only a limited number of cases. Vehicles need a yearly inspection, and a few other industrial products like steam boilers still need the TÜV seal of approval. German manufacturers nevertheless line up voluntarily, and at their own expense—the TÜVs are self-funding—to get the TÜV seal for their products. The TÜV assumes liability for products it inspects, so a user of a TÜV-inspected lawn mower who stupidly slices off a toe will have a hard time bringing a suit against the manufacturer for an alleged design defect. One can more readily imagine the plaintiff being sent off to see a TÜV psychiatrist.

In addition to liability protection, though, the TÜV also offers manufacturers a good sales pitch: "This product has been inspected by the TÜV"—that is, it's been manufactured for safety and quality. In that sense, the principle is the same as that of the Underwriters Laboratories in the United States, which puts the

UL seal of approval on products. In Germany, however, the TÜV is far more widely recognized and used: everyone, from the industrialist who wants to ensure that his factory complies with environmental regulations to the person taking a shower in a TÜV-inspected shower, can feel safer having the TÜV around.

Accounting for Success

For all of the organizing that characterizes German business, German companies remain in many ways inscrutable—a deliberate characteristic. German business is structured to encourage capital formation in such a way that companies amass—at least when business is good—vast reserves of hidden assets. When business is bad, the companies can discreetly fall back on hidden reserves, and no one is the wiser.

Under German accounting rules, companies can take far more provisions and writedowns and use rapid depreciation and anything else to show as little profit as possible. Stephen Bepler, an accountant and consultant with Capital Research International in New York, describes the German accounting system as a polite little lie between companies on the one hand and the government and labor unions on the other. "The companies say to the government, 'You can tax us at a high rate, but we get to declare lots of expenses.' It's as though the government told you that you would be taxed at a higher rate, but that you could deduct everything you needed to sustain life—your car, food, phone, home, clothes. Most people would choose that over the current system."

To illustrate how German accounting can work, Bepler cites the example of Deutsche Bank, which reportedly tried to write down its twin skyscraper headquarters in Frankfurt to one deutsche mark the day it opened. The justification: these were purpose-built buildings and of no use to anyone else. Even if this anecdote errs on the side of hyperbole, the German way is clearly designed to reduce taxable and "dividendable" earnings to a minimum. The accounting firm of KPMG Deutsche Treuhand-Gesellschaft did a comparison study in 1988 of company results for 158 German subsidiaries in the United States, using both American and German accounting principles. While the combined earnings using the American calculations came to $834 million, the total using the German method was less than half, a mere $354 million.

Indeed, corporate taxes in Germany are high—over 50 percent, compared to 34 percent in the United States and 27 percent in Britain—but effective tax reform in Germany is not just a matter of lowering the rate. Effective reform implies a fundamental shift toward greater transparency. As Bepler says, "The [current accounting] system worked well during the postwar era, when companies told people, 'This is all we earn.' But how do you segue to the truth?"

The truth is that German companies are often far more powerful than meets the eye, and the Germans like it that way. Hidden assets, they feel, are essential to maintaining the kind of stability that has brought Germany prosperity over the past forty years. The more hidden assets, the less a company is subjected to the whims of the marketplace. Why spoil a good thing by using more aggressive accounting or unlocking the hidden reserves? The windfall will only go to the government in the form of taxes or to investors in the form of dividends. Since German corporations need not fear hostile takeovers, their incentive to boost earnings —and thus the company's stock price—is very limited. Even if the German government succeeds in bringing down the tax rate, thus presumably giving companies more of an incentive to unlock hidden assets, few companies would. By the same token, few Germans would sell their umbrella in the desert—it just might rain.

With all the hidden assets squirreled away in German companies, investors in those companies have a much harder time evaluating them. Stephen Bepler knows that as well as anyone. In a speech for investors in 1990, Bepler shared the following live-and-learn experience.

I have been an analyst since 1968, and I made my first calls on international companies in 1970. The first two were Philips of Holland and Siemens of West Germany. They both sold light bulbs, but as I discovered, the similarity ended there. My experience with these two companies taught me a lesson about appearances, and more importantly, about the importance of understanding different accounting practices.

At the Philips headquarters in Eindhoven, I was cordially received in a brightly lighted room and provided with more details about the company than I could possibly remember. Philips obligingly published its reports in English and even published an addendum showing the differences between Dutch accounting standards and U.S. Generally Accepted Accounting Principles (GAAP). The atmosphere was comfortable, but just different enough to be enticing. Philips was the General Electric of Europe; at the time its stock was selling for about 45 guilders. At the end of January [1990], however—more than twenty years later—adjusting for all rights offerings, Philips was selling for only 43 guilders. So much for comfort!

My experience at Siemens, also in 1970, was totally different. In Munich, I was received in a dim room by Dr. Günter Schone, who commented that because there was ample natural light, he hoped I did not mind if he left the lights off. (It was about 3 o'clock on a gray January afternoon.) Dr. Schone proceeded to leave me in the dark about Siemens, which he consistently did to others over the years. He was cordial to a fault, but revealed virtually nothing. Siemens was then selling for about DM 165 per share. On January 31, 1990, it was selling for DM 700, adjusting for all rights offerings.

. . . Apart from the companies' very different mix of businesses, Siemens offered limited public disclosure and no guidance, and presented its results in German accounting—the analytical equivalent of Hadrian's Wall. . . . Siemens told you only what they wanted you to know, which was nothing, and were sparing even at that. Beyond this miserly level of disclosure, however, lay a dramatically undervalued equity.

Since Bepler's visit twenty years ago, not that much has changed. More German companies, including Siemens, publish annual reports in English. Corporations now have to present consolidated accounts including their foreign subsidiaries (only a few years ago, this information could be glaringly missing from the annual report). Nevertheless, the overall climate of German investor relations remains cool. Disclosure does not come naturally to Germans: they would much rather run their businesses in private —and many do.

3

Germany's Heart and Soul: The Mittelstand

Where does the secret of Germany's business success lie? If you really want to see Germany at work, take a drive through Swabia, the region of low hills and curving valleys around Stuttgart in the state of Baden-Württemberg. The locals call it Spätzle Valley, after the popular local food, and—with a tip of the hat to Silicon Valley—because the Swabians are such consummate inventors. While Stuttgart itself may be home to Germany's largest corporation, Daimler-Benz, as well as other heavies such as Bosch, SEL, Porsche and IBM Germany, Swabia is the spiritual home of the Mittelstand, the small and medium-size companies that form the true backbone of the German economy.

There's a saying in Germany: "The Swabian builds his own house." That is, he plows his resources into his private domain while refusing help from outsiders. If he has money left over, he's more likely to build a second house than to risk it all on government bonds. Stocks? To the Swabian, the word "stock" invariably implies "speculation," never "investment." And Swabia's notorious conservatism appears to have paid off: on a per capita basis Baden-Württemberg is among Germany's wealthiest states and boasts the lowest unemployment rate. Do the Swabians show off their wealth? Not at home. Stuttgart women are said to sneak their fur coats into the Mercedes while the car is still in the garage, putting them on only after the two-hour drive down to chic Munich.

Swabia never had the coal and iron that could be found in northern Germany, nor the powerful commercial advantages of the Rhine River. So the Swabians were forced to be resourceful. In the nineteenth century, their resourcefulness was given a boost by Ferdinand Steinbeis, aide to the King of Württemberg, who used public funds to foster private growth. Steinbeis made stipends available to budding entrepreneurs who wished to travel and study abroad, and bought and resold textile and other machine tools to local citizens on the condition that they show other Swabians how the machines worked. (Indeed, the tradition of strong government support lives on in Swabia: Lothar Späth, a popular conservative politician, resigned as minister of Baden-Württemberg in 1991 after word leaked out that he had been traveling on local company expense accounts. His defense? He was using his ministry to help open doors for the companies in export markets.)

Few people today remember Ferdinand Steinbeis, but everyone in Germany knows the name of Robert Bosch. An inventor of the spark plug and founder in 1866 of the company that bears his name, the legendary Bosch embodies the notion of the Swabian inventor who made good. Today the diversified auto parts manufacturer Robert Bosch GmbH is Germany's ninth largest corporation—well outside the range of the Mittelstand—yet the spirit of innovation continues.

Robert Bosch's memory lives on not just for his inventiveness but for his business philosophy. His motto, "Better to lose money than trust," still rings in the ears of many German businessmen. Bosch also considered his workers a part of his family. In 1906 he introduced the eight-hour workday in his factories, for which his industrialist contemporaries branded him "Robert the Red." When in America Henry Ford raised the wages of his workers, it was so they could better afford his cars. Bosch took the philosophy one step further, building entire housing projects and hospitals for his workers and their families.

A Working Business Ethic

In its inventiveness, its conservative business policies, its commitment to employees, Swabia typifies the Mittelstand tradition, a tradition—and an ethic—that permeates German business practice from the smallest companies to the largest multinational corporations. While the term is usually translated as "medium-size companies," "middle class" is perhaps more accurate. A German company can have over DM 1 billion in sales and thousands of employees, or be what in America passes for a "growth" company, and the owner will still tell you proudly that his company is of the Mittelstand. It's a bit like the 95 percent of all Americans who profess to belong to the same middle class. But the ethic that lies at the heart of the Mittelstand tradition is more than a "work ethic" in the usual sense of the term; rather, it represents a whole spectrum of beliefs and practices that affect every level of German business.

The Mittelstand tradition stems in great part from individual or family ownership, a structure seen by Germans as much more stable than the huge, freewheeling corporation: someone, a real person, is in charge, and thus accountable. In the eyes of many Germans, corporations are run by salaried managers and owned by anonymous shareholders whose identities can change with a keystroke on a computer. The Mittelstand company, unlike the faceless corporation, is based in a community where the owner and his employees live. The townspeople know him, the mayor comes to the company social functions and celebrations, and the company's roots might be decades—even centuries—old. A single Mittelstand company is frequently the breath of life for a small town, where the only other businesses might be a mom-and-pop grocery store, a bakery, a cleaner's. Without that Mittelstand company, the townspeople would have to drive to work elsewhere, the kids bussed to schools in bigger towns. Mittelstand companies have a heart and a soul, not just a legal existence.

The Mittelstand is also statistically significant, although numerical definitions of just what constitutes a Mittelstand company can never tell the whole story. According to German government statistics predating reunification, companies with fewer than 500 employees and sales under DM 100 million generate half the country's national production, employ two thirds of all working citizens and account for over two thirds of all exports. In the eyes of most Germans, however, this definition is too restrictive; many companies with sales in the DM 500 million range—and even some with more than DM 1 billion in sales—proudly refer to themselves as being "of the Mittelstand," if only in spirit.

It isn't its mere presence or size that makes the Mittelstand such a significant force in Germany. Virtually all highly developed countries can point to their medium-size and smaller companies as being more significant as a group than the large corporations. That might, in fact, be a good working definition of a highly developed country: a place where small business can flourish in the shadow of large corporations. Statistics for the United States and Japan, while difficult to compare because of the varying criteria for what constitutes a small or medium-size company, are not much different from those for Germany. By contrast, in a country such as South Korea, where the government is backing large conglomerates in an effort to modernize in a hurry, the impact of small and medium-size companies on the national economy is far smaller; the *chaebols,* or Korean conglomerates, account for the bulk of Korea's GNP. Yet even Korea has begun taking steps to help foster growth in medium-size and smaller companies.

But Germany is different. The extent to which German business depends on the Mittelstand is incalculable. Take autos, perhaps Germany's most famous product after beer. The German automobile industry depends heavily on the high quality and prompt service of its suppliers, many of them Mittelstand companies. An average car requires thousands of parts, each more technically complicated than the last. And every year the cars come in different styles, while the expensive options of yesteryear become the standard features of today. Carmakers have learned to keep their inventory costs down by manufacturing on the just-in-time principle, which places tremendous pressure on suppliers to deliver quality goods precisely when they're needed. Not surprisingly, companies good enough to supply Mercedes-Benz and Volkswagen also supply carmakers around the world, such as GM, Honda and Fiat. And those suppliers are typically of the Mittelstand.

Examples?

Hella KG Hueck & Co., based in Lippstadt, is one of Europe's market leaders for headlights and other reflectors. Controlled 100 percent by the Hueck family, the company has assets of over DM 800 million. As is typical for a German Mittelstand company, equity and reserves comfortably exceed debt. Hella's biggest clients include Volkswagen, Mercedes-Benz, Ford, Renault and Fiat. Smaller clients include Chrysler, Toyota and Nissan, among others.

Brose Fahrzeugteile GmbH & Co. KG, based in Coburg near the old border of East Germany, is also 100 percent family-owned. This manufacturer of electric windows and seat adjusters supplies Jaguar, Mercedes-Benz, Saab, Toyota, Volvo and twenty other automobile manufacturers. Sales total over DM 700 million.

In Stuttgart, Dürr GmbH, a subsidiary of a publicly quoted holding company whose voting control is in the hands of Heinz Dürr and his family, manufactures paint shop machines for auto producers around the world. Sales exceed DM 400 million.

The list could go on. Suffice it to say that a lot of German families make a comfortable living off the nearly trillion-dollar worldwide auto industry.

The Ethic of the Niche Market

The secret of the Mittelstand lies in the strength of its collective business and personal ethic, which controls much of the way its business gets done—from its strong preference for the niche market to its insistence on privacy and control to its sense of social commitment, and beyond. Indeed, the notion of the Mittelstand is as much defined by that ethic as it is by size, wealth or any other statistic.

The Mittelstand ethic has at its base the fact that the Mittelstand company is usually the exclusive domain of its owner, who will brook no outside interference from investors and banks unless he is forced to. That's not to say the owner is a ruthless tyrant. Normally he is as attached to his employees as a father is to his children. Many companies function more like patriarchies than like corporations. Thus, the truest measure of success for a Mittelstand owner is to pass a bulletproof balance sheet on to a son. (If nature has been cruel and provided daughters only, a son-in-law will usually do.) The contrast with the United States, where entrepreneurial success is defined by the ability to build up a company and take it public, is marked.

Perhaps the best example of the Mittelstand ethic as business practice is its strong preference for niche markets. And perhaps the best example of German dominance of a niche market is its machine tool trade. Names like Trumpf, Karl Mayer and Voith are known to their customers around the world for their quality laser cutting tools, knitting machines and paper-making machines, respectively. Visit their factories, and you see a remarkable German machine matrix: German-made machines being used to make more German-made machines. Plenty of German machines are also sold outside the matrix, since exports are almost always in excess of 50 percent, and often as high as 80 percent or 90 percent, of a company's sales. As a whole, German Mittelstand machine tool companies employ 1.1 million workers, more than any other sector of the economy, including automobile manufacturing.

Of course, the machine tool matrix isn't the only outlet for German machine tool companies. Indeed, the Mittelstand also stands behind many consumer products familiar worldwide, though few are aware of the abiding influence of this sector of the German economy. Americans have all heard of Mercedes-Benz and Volkswagen—but Körber AG? Krones AG?

Körber, based in Hamburg, is the world's leading producer of rolling machines used by cigarette manufacturers such as R. J. Reynolds and Philip Morris. About nine out of every ten filter cigarettes are rolled up in a Körber machine. Aren't cigarettes a dying industry? Perhaps, but the Körber technology, which accounts for over half of the company's annual DM 1.5 billion in sales, can also be used for rolling tampons. Furthermore, the company is diversified: a quarter of its sales stems from machine tools for the auto industry (clients include Mercedes-Benz, BMW and Ford) and the rest from the paper industry (Mead Papers, 3M, Fuji-Xerox). Of these sales, over 80 percent are exports. Founded by Kurt Körber just after the war, the company remains owned by him and a nonprofit foundation he created.

Krones is another invisible German presence behind some of the most recognizable brands in the world. Based just outside Regensburg on the Danube, Krones does most of its DM 830 million in sales selling bottle-labeling machines to hundreds of German breweries as well as worldwide heavyweights such as Anheuser-Busch, Gallo, Heinz and others. Using the latest in computer-aided design and manufacturing technology, Krones technicians design the shape of a client's label on a screen, then press a button. Down on the factory floor, ultra-high-pressure water jets begin cutting the plastic mold that presses the glue-coated label onto the bottle. It's not a totally high-tech industry like semiconductors, but because of the high precision required, it's awfully close.

Within Germany there are critics who contend that the country is being left behind in the industries of the future like computers or microelectronics. But at Krones, the industries of the future are being used to build products for today. What's more, these products turn a profit. Muses Volker Kronseder, the vice president and son of the company founder, "Our business does well in good times and in bad. When the client's business is off, they usually figure that the product is fine and that just the label design needs changing." Kronseder remembers with satisfaction the U.S. government mandate that beer bottles carry a label warning pregnant mothers of the risk of alcohol: the company picked up a few extra million deutsche marks in sales.

Although, like most companies, Mittelstand firms have growth as their objective, the pursuit of the niche often limits that growth. There are exceptions. The Bertelsmann publishing empire was a small, fifth-generation publishing house when Reinhard Mohn built it into a multi-billion-deutsche-mark company. The same is true of the Otto Versand mail-order house, founded by Werner Otto shortly after the war and today the world's leading catalog company—bigger even than Sears. Most of the classic Mittelstand companies, however, would rather avoid the mass market, which has the greatest growth potential but also the fiercest competition, preferring instead to focus on specialized products that only a handful of competitors will bother to make.

When it comes to occupying a niche, perhaps no company has it better than the Karl Mayer Textilmaschinenfabrik GmbH. "For most of our textile machines, we have no competition," claims Fritz Mayer, son of company founder Karl. The senior Mayer built his first knitting machine for producing textiles in 1948 and later added machines for making lace and curtain fabrics. Today the company produces specialized machinery for every conceivable specialized fabric, from the windscreen behind a tennis court to elastic stretch pants to the upholstery on a car seat to terrycloth towels.

Much of the company's success is due to its aggressive export policy, which started soon after the company was founded. In the early 1950s Karl Mayer was exporting to the United States; by 1955 he had established his first U.S. subsidiary, in New Jersey. Taking advantage of the then-favorable exchange rate of DM 4 to $1, Mayer kept prices low and service high, and his only U.S. competitor soon went out of business. Meanwhile, exports to Japan began in 1954. Production there followed in the 1960s, when the company took a stake in a competitor, which it bought out entirely in 1968. Several years later it also bought out the only other Japanese competitor. Today the company exports well over 80 percent of production, with the only substantial competition coming from one other West German firm.

How does Karl Mayer do it? "It's more the material than the machines," says Fritz Mayer. "Many products can only be made on our machines." Take lace. In America, 90 percent of all lace starts out as threads on a Karl Mayer machine. (Fritz Mayer points out that the difficult period of the mid-1970s for the company was exacerbated by women going without bras, thus reducing the demand for lace.) The textiles used to make many types of curtains or stretch bicycle shorts can often be made only on Karl Mayer machines.

To keep abreast of fabrics, the company actively participates in the initial fiber development as well as the subsequent use of a fiber to manufacture fabrics. Karl Mayer sells machines to fiber manufacturers such as Hoechst that allow them to produce the fibers, then sells the knitting machines that turn those fibers into fabric to textile mills like Milliken in South Carolina, the largest in the United States. Over 10 percent of company sales goes to research and development, with a good portion of that devoted to fabric research. As in all German companies, training is emphasized. Technicians from all over the world come to spend six months learning from dawn to dusk about the machines.

Other aspects of Karl Mayer's Mittelstand ethic are easy to spot. Workers on their way into the Obertshausen plant can look right into the windows of the ground floor and see Fritz Mayer and his two brothers, Ulrich and Ingo, at work in their adjoining offices. The offices are separated by shoulder-high plate-glass windows: if Fritz decides his putting stroke needs a little practice, Ulrich, Ingo and any passerby would have ringside seats for the practice session. When this family goes to work, they come to work. Fritz Mayer, who started at the company when he was fifteen, says that even as a young child he knew he'd be working there. Nor has he any doubt that some day one or more of Karl Mayer's eleven grandchildren will take over.

The family doesn't try to impress visitors with lavish head-quarters; their financial statements are impressive enough: a profit margin of roughly 10 percent on sales of DM 500 million, and no bank debt. "If the banks offer us anything, it's usually a higher interest rate for us to place our money," says Fritz Mayer with a smile. But, as he points out, the company often puts its money on the line to finance customers, making a stable reserve essential.

Shortly after the Berlin Wall came down, the company rushed knitting machines—originally destined for other customers—to clients in East Germany so they could remain competitive. That was risky, but not unusual. "We were financing customers in Brazil in the early 1980s when no one else would even go near the country," says Fritz Mayer. How does the company evaluate the risk? "It's mostly a feeling about the person, so we always try to find people like us who own and operate their own companies. [About 80 percent of Karl Mayer customers fall into that category.] Our clients know that we stand by them better than most banks."

Of course, it takes luck for a company like Karl Mayer to have found a niche where it has no competition for a majority of its products. Many Mittelstand companies compete in markets with razor-thin margins and unpredictable economic cycles. But even they try to find room in their production for products so specialized that competitors have no interest in entering the field. High specialization usually requires building the component parts in the factory and relying as little as possible on outside suppliers. That in turn requires a skilled labor force that only apprenticeships and ongoing investment in training can provide. The Mittelstand ethic is indeed woven deeply into Germany's business and social fabric.

The Ethic of Private Control

In addition to belief in the value of niche markets, the Mittelstand ethic can be defined by its preference for private ownership or control. There's more to it than an "I'm the boss" attitude, although nothing ever gets done without the owner's approval. The owner is bound to the business for the long haul, just as the business is bound to him. He doesn't think of maximizing short-term gains if it will harm the company's long-term chances for success, and private control ensures that outside interference will be minimal. Tradition is more than a slogan to be used in advertising.

While the surest way to ensure tradition and continuity is to keep the company private, the German owner typically takes this one step further. The overwhelming majority (80 percent) of Mittelstand companies are personally held, according to the Institute for Mittelstand Research in Bonn, thus putting all the risk on the shoulders of the owner. "The Mittelstand owner doesn't always act rationally," says Günter Kayser, the head of the institute. "He sometimes identifies too strongly with his company. This individualism leads him to look for family members to succeed him at the expense of qualified managers. And if the owner goes bankrupt, it is a total blow to his reputation. Not like in America [where,] depending on the circumstances of how they went under, they may be able to start over."

On the other hand, as Kayser points out, "The head of a Mittelstand company has, and rightly so, the same sense of self-worth as the head of Daimler-Benz. It's not like in Japan, where the smaller the company, the lower the sense of esteem."

Most of the larger Mittelstand companies choose from a wide range of corporate organizational forms that nevertheless ensure private control. Some companies, such as Hella, are set up as limited partnerships (KG), while others, such as Karl Mayer, choose to incorporate with limited liability (GmbH). Even those companies that have fully incorporated into an *Aktiengesellschaft* (AG) are frequently not publicly quoted, like Körber, or, as in the case of Krones, float only nonvoting shares on the market, keeping all the voting shares in the family.

The Mittelstand owner frequently chooses privacy as well as private control. Most Germans find financial disclosure about as desirable as standing naked on a street corner. Only belatedly has the German government stepped up disclosure requirements, and that over heated opposition from Mittelstand owners. Not until a few years ago did a limited liability corporation (GmbH) with sales of over DM 400 million have to publish an income statement. It's not unusual for companies to pay the fine for nondisclosure rather than expose themselves. A more cumbersome—but effective—tactic is used by the billionaire Albrecht brothers, Karl and Theo, and their Aldi chain of discount supermarkets. Like a bee colony, their company spins off new partnerships as it grows; each partnership's total sales, employees and assets never exceed the disclosure threshold. At last count, their German supermarket empire numbered over thirty-two separate GmbH & Co. KG entities.

The notorious GmbH & Co. KG is an exclusively—and typically—German creation that allows limited disclosure since it's a partnership (the KG part), while avoiding unlimited liability for the general partner since the general partner is a corporation (the GmbH part). The European Community has pressured the German government to mandate greater disclosure in these companies, so privacy-obsessed Germans will have to find other ways to remain invisible.

The German predisposition toward privacy can be explained in part by the threat of kidnapping or terrorism. In 1971, for example, Theo Albrecht was held for ransom. As recently as 1989 a car bomb took the life of Deutsche Bank head Alfred Herrhausen. In April 1991 a sniper shot and killed Detlev Rohwedder, head of the Treuhandanstalt, the agency responsible for privatizing former East German businesses. Still, such threats are statistically improbable, and no Mittelstand owner could possibly spend all his time worrying about kidnapping. An even greater impetus to privacy lies in the no-win situation every successful German businessman faces: If business is bad, he'll have problems with customers who will question if his company is on solid ground. If business is good, he'll be the subject of envy.

"Envy" is a word that comes up repeatedly when describing the German psyche. The sentiment is so rooted in German culture that the language provides two words to describe it: *Neid* and *Mißgunst*. Magazines run cover stories with titles like "Update on Envy: What the Germans Feel." As Volker Kronseder of Krones AG puts it, "If you have more than the next guy, he thinks you must have done something wrong to get it." Germans are only beginning to learn to live with their wealth out in the open. It's not like in America, where the rich are celebrated. In Germany, having a successful company and the wealth that comes along with it is a double-edged sword.

All that envy should come as no surprise, considering the great wealth produced by Mittelstand companies. When *!Forbes von Burda* first published its list of the 400 richest Germans in 1990— single-handedly raising the envy level throughout the country to an all-time high—an overwhelming majority of the individual and family fortunes were tied to the Mittelstand. The Kronseders, Mayers, Leibingers, Stihls and many other owners mentioned in this chapter made it onto the *!Forbes von Burda* list. Yet they invariably downplay the significance of their appearance on the list, insisting that all their money is tied up in the company. They worry that the average German will think they don't work for a living or that they live like the sultan of Brunei. Or even worse, that the unions will be that much more aggressive in the next round of salary negotiations.

The contrast between the wealthy in Germany and in America is marked. Wealthy Americans make their money many different ways: stock ownership, real estate, dealmaking, oil and so on. Wealthy Germans typically make their fortunes over time through private ownership of a going concern.

The Ethic of Commitment

Mittelstand owners are widely respected in Germany, and their
authority in the social market economy cannot be underestimated.
"When a Mittelstand owner comments on business, his words
often carry more weight than do those of a salaried employee of a
corporation," says Ulrich Hermani, whose boss, Berthold Leibinger, is the majority owner and chief executive officer of Trumpf
GmbH. Of course, that has to be put into perspective. Clearly,
the head of Deutsche Bank doesn't have to shout from the top of
the twin towers in Frankfurt to make himself heard in Bonn.
Nevertheless, the Mittelstand owner commands a certain amount
of respect in Germany simply because he alone takes the risk of
doing business and because his interests are indistinguishable from
the long-term interests of his company.

One illustration of this respect is the fact that the heads of
many of Germany's influential trade associations come from the
ranks of the Mittelstand. These associations don't exist to serve as
an excuse for annual conventions in Monte Carlo. They are democratically governed bodies that serve as a vital link between the
business world and the government or the unions.

The Bundesverband der Deutschen Industrie (BDI) is an umbrella group for various industrial associations. The BDI might
consult with the government on matters like export verification
measures, as was the case after it was discovered that German
firms had shipped equipment to Iraq that could be transformed
into war materiel. In the Presidium of the BDI are often the heads
of large public corporations like Carl Hahn of Volkswagen or
Karlheinz Kaske of Siemens, but the president of the BDI is almost always drawn from the ranks of the Mittelstand. The current leader is Heinrich Weiss, whose company, SMS Schloemann-
Siemag AG, builds turnkey steel mills and provides the steel
industry with other machinery. Trumpf's Berthold Leibinger,
who also sits on the BDI Presidium, is at the same time the head
of the German machine builders' association, the Verband Deutscher Maschinen- und Anlagenbau. Hans Peter Stihl, who heads
the chain saw manufacturer Andreas Stihl, based in Waiblingen
just outside of Stuttgart, is also the head of another important
association, the Deutscher Industrie- und Handelstag (DIHT).

Why do these men agree to devote as much as 20 percent of their precious time to such matters? "It's more than just an honor," explains Leibinger. "It's almost an obligation." The associations don't have much power per se, but their influence is substantial. Every few weeks, Chancellor Helmut Kohl invites the heads of the more important associations to discuss current topics. During the early stages of German reunification, for example, Kohl met with Leibinger and others to get a clearer picture of what measures were needed to spur investment in eastern Germany. When Kohl saw that investment would be slow to materialize from private industry, he called on the Federal Republic's member states to pony up the necessary funds.

Whether the trade association head is schmoozing with Chancellor Kohl or developing common industrial standards, the authority is not nearly as rigid as is, say, the relationship between Japan's MITI and Japanese companies. In Germany a company does not have to belong to an association. Karl Mayer, for example, has chosen not to join the textile machine association. "We prefer to represent our products ourselves and have nothing to gain from the association," says Fritz Mayer.

Nevertheless, the participation of leading Mittelstand owners and other corporate executives gives most German trade associations more influence than their counterparts in the United States. The way American business communicates with the government is more often through a paid lobbyist or perhaps a close personal friend of the president, a cabinet secretary or a congressman. In Germany the consultation is within the framework of a system. It's fairer that way, the Germans think. The association head is democratically elected, so that even the smallest member is represented, whereas in the United States the firms with the most money can afford the best lobbyists.

The Mittelstand Abroad

Because the German Mittelstand is so well supported and represented at home, it's no wonder that many choose to do all their production in Germany and then export. Not always, however: larger Mittelstand companies like Karl Mayer, Krones and Körber often must follow the markets and have successfully established production outside of the Fatherland. But other Mittelstand companies aren't always so lucky. Without the resources of a large corporation with its squads of specialists and legal advisors, the margin of error can be terribly thin.

Walter Lindenmaier always loved America. The freedom he felt when he was there even led his wife and him to arrange to be in the United States when each of their three children was born: he wanted the kids to have both German and American nationality. That was back in the mid-1970s, when the vogue of Euro-pessimism was at its height. Europe was being rocked by the oil crisis, and the Russians were still just over the horizon to the east. America looked like the safest haven. But when Lindenmaier figured he'd finally try to do business in America, it turned out to be a great deal harder than he thought. Now he's back to loving America solely as a tourist.

Lindenmaier is the third generation to manage the Lindenmaier Präzision AG, based in Laupheim, just south of Ulm. The company has sales of around DM 125 million from the manufacture of machine tools as well as over 250 different types of precision metal parts. Many of these small parts sell for as little as DM 1 and are used by the automobile industry to make fuel pumps and the like. It's a fiercely competitive business: the big auto companies and large parts makers like Bosch can drive an awfully hard bargain. Still, Lindenmaier had turned a good profit for years, and in 1983 he transformed the company into a stock company with an eye to going public someday.

"I also wanted to build something in America," recalls Lindenmaier. He started out well enough in 1988 with an office that sold his and other machines to American clients. Then he got an order from the Dana Corporation in Bristol, Connecticut, for three machines that make gearbox parts. As Lindenmaier tells it, "There were no machines on the market anywhere that would perform the desired function, and the American I had chosen to head the subsidiary said, 'No problem, we can do it.' I lost so much money in America because everybody told me they could do it, and they couldn't do anything. Americans are big improvisors. They patch things together, but there's no dependability. Look at their cars. The car runs, but it's not a quality product. I wonder if it has to be. Probably not, but that's how we make them, because we can't do it differently."

Lindenmaier lost millions on the machines for Dana. He even had to replace malfunctioning parts ordered by his American subsidiary. But his American business nightmare wasn't over. In 1989, one of his biggest customers, the auto parts manufacturer Bosch, suggested he manufacture metal brake parts in America. Bosch was trying to spruce up its "Made in America" image with as much local content as possible. Lindenmaier agreed, and his American president floated an industrial revenue bond to raise the money for the machines to produce the parts. Getting the money was easy, but Lindenmaier had trouble getting the machines to his American subsidiary in time. So Bosch turned in part to other suppliers. Without the hoped-for volume, Lindenmaier wasn't breaking even, so he decided to sell the American business entirely. To do so, he first had to get out from under the bond. "The bond books were five thousand pages long. No one had had time to read them." As it turned out, Lindenmaier needed approval from at least six different parties, including the Connecticut bond advisor, the remarketing agent and various banks. "It took twenty-nine lawyers," he says with incredulity, "and that was only to sell the company assets. In America you have to spell out everything. Here we don't have that problem. In the end I had to pay a bank an extra two hundred thousand dollars just to get their approval," he concludes with disgust.

Does Lindenmaier think Americans can do business in Germany? "No. The cultures are too different," says Lindenmaier. Illustrating the point with Brechtian theatricality, he props his feet up on the table and lounges back in his chair. "In America people don't think anything of doing this. In Germany we just can't."

Yet the Mittelstand must continue to think about the world outside the Fatherland. Markets are expanding constantly, and the possibility of producing overseas is always there—eastern Germany, Eastern Europe, even Asia.

If the Mittelstand is going to profit from the reunification with East Germany, it will come more from selling products to the East and less from producing with cheap labor there. Besides, the risks associated with producing in the East are more easily borne by deep-pocketed corporations. On the other hand, the sales potential within eastern Germany is going to benefit plenty of smaller German firms. The window maker can get into his car and drive around, find houses in need of better windows, and make sales with a minimum of risk. For every time a major corporation announces a big investment somewhere in eastern Germany, getting itself written up in the papers, ten Mittelstand companies will no doubt have already made a sale.

The German Mittelstand has been heavily concentrated in export markets for years, so the much-talked-about opening of new markets in the eastern German "backyard" is taken in stride. "I don't see why just because we have five new states I should go [produce] there," says Walter Lindenmaier, still shell-shocked from his dismal experience in America. "Some of my competitors have said they will go. They should go. But it's much too early. Besides, there is still plenty to do here."

"All markets are important," says Fritz Mayer of the Karl Mayer company. "But if anything, we feel that Asia is one of the most important. I'll fly to Korea for the day if I have to in order to sell a machine. Last year our business was down in the United States and much of Europe. Only through better-than-usual business in Germany and in Asia were we able to achieve a higher volume overall." The importance of Asia is echoed by Berthold Leibinger of Trumpf, who also flies there routinely, and who calls on his fellow German entrepreneurs to increase their presence in Southeast Asia.

The future is one subject most Mittelstand owners don't have time to worry about. They are too busy with the present. "We don't have a ten-year plan, or a five-year plan or a two-year plan," insists Mayer. Yet Germans are worried that the younger generation is less and less willing to work sixty hours in daddy's plant when they can work only thirty-eight in the local bank. Because many of today's Mittelstand companies were founded in the immediate postwar period, the second generation is slowly giving way to a third. With each successive generation, ownership and management transfer becomes more difficult. Cousins may fight for control, or no one may—the hunger may have left the family entirely. Either way, the prospect of selling out is gaining added appeal. Enter the buyout firms, with their slick brochures explaining how they work for the long-term interests of the company, and how it's the other guys who are out to make a quick deutsche mark. But theirs is still a tough job. "We were interested in one Mittelstand company," says one buyout specialist backed by deep pockets, "but the owner wanted four times what we were willing to pay."

And don't believe the inevitable reports that the younger German generation has gone the way of the Roman Empire, despite talk of German yuppies and the *Schickeria,* the idle rich. Late one night in a Munich bar, Hanns Martin (those are his first names) explains that he is studying mechanical engineering. Naturally he is from Stuttgart. "I have an idea for a machine. I want to get a patent. It's not a very complicated machine. But I think it will work. I want to work all the time, as long as it's for me." Wealth creation in Germany will not come to a grinding halt in the near future. And the Mittelstand—and all it stands for—will be at the heart of any new wealth created.

4

Bank on It:
Germany's Universal
Banking System

Any discussion of German business invariably turns sooner
or later to the subject of German banks. Under the so-called universal banking system, German banks are allowed to engage in
every conceivable financial activity—and they do. Commercial
banking, investment banking, merchant banking, asset management, insurance—German banks have a hand in virtually every
transaction inside the country.

The issue of banking power in Germany has long titillated
the press and other observers of German business. The banks
appear to have the German economy firmly in their grasp. Woe-

fully few German companies bother to go public or seek any type of financing more complicated than a straight bank loan. All of the leading banks hold vast ownership stakes in German industrial companies, while German bankers dominate the ranks of even more company supervisory boards. Even allowing for the relative weakness of German supervisory boards compared with the management boards, it is safe to say that German banks occupy an extremely powerful position in the German business world.

Deutsche Bank über Alles

As Germany's leading bank, Deutsche Bank exemplifies the towering position of the banks in the German economy. Deutsche Bank holds a 28 percent stake in Germany's leading industrial company, Daimler-Benz, as well as 10 percent of the country's leading insurance company, Allianz; another 10 percent of the largest reinsurance company, Munich Re; a 25 percent stake in the country's leading department store chain, Karstadt; nearly one third of the leading German construction company, Philipp Holzmann; and a dozen or more stakes in other leading blue-chip companies. The leading bankers from Deutsche Bank, meanwhile, can be found on the supervisory and various ad hoc advisory boards of over 150 companies.

Deutsche Bank's influence over German business is unparalleled in any other country. Attempts at comparison invariably fall short. In the United States, Citibank would have to own a significant chunk of General Motors as well as stakes in dozens of other major firms and have investment banking operations on a par with the likes of Morgan Stanley just to come close.

The close ties that Deutsche and the other German banks have forged with industry go back over one hundred years. Industrialization came late to Germany, and large pools of privately held capital simply didn't exist, so German banks stepped in to fill the gap. Deutsche Bank's first chief executive, in 1870, was Georg von Siemens, a cousin of Werner von Siemens, founder of the electrical company that still bears his name.

The close relationship between banking and industry continued well into this century. Hermann Josef Abs, who guided the bank through the tumult of World War II, also helped restore the bank's preeminence after the war through his own close ties to industry. Abs, who looked and acted the part of the consummate discreet banker, held so many supervisory and other advisory board positions—at one time over thirty—that in 1965 the German legislature voted what is still known in Germany as the "Lex Abs." Under the law, no one can hold supervisory board positions in more than ten "Aktiengesellschaft" at one time.

More recently, before he was blown up by a terrorist car bomb in November 1989, Alfred Herrhausen personified the power of Deutsche Bank for all to see—no doubt one reason the lunatics from the Red Army Faction terrorist organization found him such a desirable target. Unlike Abs, the mediagenic Herrhausen was never one to shy away from publicity. His lean, rugged good looks led one female biographer to compare him to the French movie star Alain Delon. One minute he was advising Chancellor Helmut Kohl on monetary issues, the next he was giving a speech before an international banking conference, then flying off to London to buy up the venerable Morgan Grenfell brokerage house, then "back in Germany in time for lunch," as the British press described in awe.

But Herrhausen was more than a banker; he was an industrial strategist. He knew industry from his days at the Vereinigte Elektrizitätswerke Westfalen AG (VEW) utility, where he was chief financial officer. At Deutsche Bank, he busied himself with several issues affecting industry. No doubt his biggest deal came shortly after he took over the post of supervisory board chairman for Daimler-Benz in 1988.

Herrhausen helped ease Werner Breitschwerdt, then Daimler-Benz's CEO, into an early retirement in order to make room for Edzard Reuter, who was more receptive to Herrhausen's ideas for diversifying the automotive company. Under Reuter, Daimler acquired, among other companies, the Munich-based arms and aerospace concern Messerschmitt-Bölkow-Blohm, while Herrhausen used his political connections to get the deal approved by the government over the objections of the country's monopolies commission (whether this deal was worth the trouble is another question).

Deploying the Forces

Clearly, German bankers have a lot of clout. Looking at the stakes banks hold in industrial companies and the seats they occupy on company supervisory boards, one might easily infer that the German banks, like master puppeteers, pull all the strings of German industry. Deutsche Bank seems to have the most strings and the most puppets, but all the large German banks play the game.

The power of the bank stakes is augmented by German corporate law, which gives minority shareholders considerable rights. If a public company wants to change its capital structure, perhaps by issuing new shares or by floating new bonds, over 75 percent of all shareholders must approve. Thus a bank that holds a 25 percent stake has what is known as a blocking minority.

And the German proxy system gives the banks added punch. Banks are allowed to act as stockbrokers, and they can vote shares deposited in their accounts if the real shareholder has not made his voting intentions known. Most German stockholders, like stockholders everywhere, throw their proxy statements into the trash without bothering to fill them out. Thus the banks often wind up voting more shares than their nominal holding in a company might indicate.

In many ways, however, the bank stakes in industrial companies and the bankers' seats on supervisory boards are more a reflection of bank power than the instruments of that power. The real reason banks have influence and power is that when it comes to business and money, the private, conservative German psyche has for years played right into the hands of the banks.

Consider the strict anti-inflationary policies of the German central bank, the Bundesbank. German depositors love being able to deposit their hard-earned deutsche marks at the bank for long periods without worrying about keeping up with inflation. The banks, meanwhile, get to pay out low, low interest on the deposits without having to pursue speculative loans. This arrangement pleases the frugal Germans immensely, although foreigners don't always like the consequences of the Bundesbank's dogmatically anti-inflationary ways.

Early in 1991 the European commissioner from England, Roy Jenkins, said that the Bundesbank had replaced the German army as "the quintessential German institution." The German central bank had just raised interest rates because of inflationary fears related to the cost of German reunification, even as other European countries were trying to lower their rates to stimulate more economic activity. As usual, though, the complaint fell on deaf ears. Germans have suffered enough monetary chaos in this century—the hyperinflation of 1923 and again just prior to the 1948 currency reform—to criticize their central bank too strongly.

Thrift and savings are classic German virtues, and at least since the end of the war Germans have for the most part put their savings into passbook savings accounts, not stocks or bonds. The trend is away from these passbook accounts, but even today one can find savings accounts paying as low as 2.5 percent interest and requiring three months' notice before any withdrawals can be made. Germans trust their banks, and they believe in compound interest. The government has helped by turning a blind eye when Germans "forget" to declare interest income for tax purposes. In 1989 the government introduced a 10 percent withholding tax on interest income, but nervous depositors began taking trunkloads of cash over the border into Luxembourg; needless to say, the plan was quickly scrapped. A new withholding tax is in the works, but it will have generous interest income exemptions.

As for borrowing, postwar Germany has been the land of commercial banking, although that is slowly beginning to change. A company typically developed a relationship with a "house bank" and did not experiment with fancy financial products—just loans. Even at many of the large corporations, the corporate treasurer was more likely to go with a standard loan than a cheaper product like commercial paper. The rationale: by paying more for the bank loan, the company was buying insurance that the bank would stand by it in a pinch.

Some bank critics argue that the banks discourage companies from going public so they can continue to feed them loans and live off the interest payments. While this charge is vigorously denied by the banks, the truth lies somewhere in between. The large banks offer investment banking as well as commercial banking, and what they lose on the commercial end they can presumably make up in underwriting fees. But sometimes this presumption falls flat. The local branch manager who makes commercial loans is not eager to turn his best client over to the invest-ment banking boys back in Frankfurt. So the client does not always receive impartial advice from the bank. Then there are the small banks: with no investment banking activities, they have nothing to gain and everything to lose if their client decides to go public.

Nevertheless, the banks cannot be entirely blamed for the dearth of publicly quoted German companies. The German Mit-telstand owner is often so proud of carrying on the family tradi-tion that he would never go public, a notion that to him resembles selling his very soul. Getting loans from the bank also offers the advantage of raising capital without having to disclose the condi-tion of the company—and his own wealth—to the public.

In addition, many Mittelstand companies are structured as limited partnerships, and the tax laws work against their transfor-mation into public corporations. A person inheriting a building owned by a limited partnership is taxed at only 5 percent to 10 percent of its market value, whereas the same person inheriting a share of a public corporation is taxed on the full value of the property.

Most Germans simply figure that the power of the German banks and their dominant role are the price to be paid for stability. Alfred Herrhausen once responded to a question about the power of German banks by saying, "I have never been one to deny that [Deutsche Bank] has power. The question is not whether we have power, but rather how we handle it and whether we use it respon-sibly or not." Precisely. Germans may complain now and then that their banks have too much power, but when they look at the freewheeling financial markets of the United States—the savings-and-loan disaster, government bailouts of large banks, rampant greed on Wall Street, leveraged buyouts, hostile takeovers, junk bonds—they count their blessings.

For all their power, German banks do occasionally act with some restraint. Many of the bank stakes in industrial companies are the result of rescue operations, when a troubled company has appealed to the banks for capital. The banks oblige, and in return take an equity stake in the company. The method costs the com-pany less than an emergency loan and allows more time for a turnaround. Deutsche Bank and Commerzbank both have stakes in Karstadt AG, for example, the origins of which go back to the depression era of the 1930s, when the retailer was nearly bankrupt. More recently, Deutsche Bank rescued Klöckner-Humboldt-Deutz AG, and still holds over 40 percent of the company's stock.

The German banks are also hostile to hostile takeovers, again not surprising considering how much the Germans love stability. The bankers are not about to sell their stakes in companies to a takeover artist interested only in a quick profit. On the contrary, as we shall see, the bank stakes in an industrial firm make for excellent shark repellent. Furthermore, the banks have been reducing their industrial holdings and might be more inclined to sell off more if the high German capital gains tax rate—50 percent on some investments—were reduced. Many of the bank holdings, like Karstadt, were acquired at a low cost years before.

Finally, if German bankers sit in unequaled numbers on supervisory boards, it's for a simple reason: they are asked to by the companies themselves. What better way for a company to announce to the world that it has a steady line of credit than to have a banker on the board?

If German banks sit atop the world of German business, it's not necessarily because they clawed their way up there on the backs of unwilling Germans. And, as many German bankers are quick to point out, they don't even have a complete lock on their own business.

More and more industrial companies are offering financial services, robbing the banks of part of their traditional business. As in the United States, the acute competition with the banks comes from the automobile companies (although, as one German car dealer points out, many of his customers prefer to get a bank loan and then show up with wads of cash and an eye for a discount). Deutsche Bank owns 28 percent of Daimler-Benz, controls the company's supervisory board and went out of its way to put Edzard Reuter in the chief executive's chair, none of which prevented Reuter from establishing a separate consumer financing division for buyers of Mercedes cars and other Daimler products.

Deutsche Bank also faces stiff competition for depositors. The post office, with its extensive branch network, also offers banking

services. More troublesome for the banks are insurance companies, which in recent years have gained ever-increasing portions
of German savings. This competition poses a dilemma for the
banks, since insurance companies are among their largest allies
when it comes to investing in stocks and bonds underwritten by
the banks. Deutsche Bank and Allianz, the two giants of their
respective industries, had always tried to keep from stepping on
each other's toes. After a few years of hand wringing, however,
Deutsche finally decided to enter the life insurance field in 1989.
Not surprisingly, Allianz as well as other insurers have trimmed
some of their investment business with the bank.

The German Advantage

The German universal banking system, while clearly giving banks
a great deal of power, nevertheless has its advantages, and these
advantages have been noticed outside of Germany. In the spring
of 1990, Ulrich Cartellieri, a member of the management board
of Deutsche Bank, traveled to Washington, D.C., to enlighten a
panel of senators on the virtues of the German banking system,
and to meet informally with officials in the Treasury Department.

Banking authorities in the United States have been anxiously
trying to shore up their troubled banking system, and not long
after Cartellieri's visit, U.S. Treasury Secretary Nicholas Brady
proposed a dramatic overhaul of the banking system. The proposed legislation, which would have allowed banks to engage in
both commercial and investment banking, was defeated by Congress the first time around for a variety of reasons, but the idea of
opening up a wider range of business in which American banks
can compete is far from dead.

Back in Düsseldorf, from his second-floor office overlooking
the fashionable Königsallee, Cartellieri reiterates why he feels the
universal banking system is superior. In the United States, he
points out, restricting banks to either investment or commercial
banking has forced the institutions to specialize more and more in
order to remain competitive. An American investment bank may
be the best bond underwriter, but if interest rates turn up and the
bank is stuck with the bonds in its portfolio, the entire investment

bank's equity can be wiped out. "Our banks may not be the strongest in any one area," says Cartellieri, "but overall they perform well because they have a cushion if one area turns bad."

Cartellieri also makes a persuasive argument that the universal system is the best way to attack the largest structural problem affecting banking, be it in the United States or in Germany: the oversupply of banks. Cartellieri cites the comments of one industrialist who pointed out that banks are going to be the steel industry of the 1990s, adding, "We need to find a way for banks to drop out of the system. If not bankruptcy, given the repercussions on the rest of the economy, then diversification."

Listening to Cartellieri, one comes to appreciate that the strength of German banking is not just in its structure, but also in the heads of bankers. German bankers act the part, and are never comfortable with any upstart who goes too far, too fast, too loud. "I have to wonder when I see bankers of the first league in the United States lend to a man like Donald Trump," says Cartellieri in his near-perfect English. "I hope such a bird never takes wings in Germany." One might point out that the American branch of Germany's Commerzbank lent to Trump, but then again, the German bank was the first to want to leave Trump hanging when it became clear he was overleveraged. The other lenders opted to restructure the Trump holdings.

In Germany, there was the case of Horst-Dieter Esch, who in the early 1980s borrowed a lot of money fast to buy up a string of machine tool companies. In that case, however, Esch got his financing not from the large establishment banks, but from the private bank of Schröder, Münchmeyer, Hengst, which bypassed the legal lending limits via a Luxembourg subsidiary. Esch's empire crumbled in the recession of 1983, the private bank had to be bailed out and the German banking establishment saw one more demonstration of how it pays to be prudent.

With their vast concentration of power, Germany's large banks are clearly too big to fail. Germans are naturally inclined to reduce the risk through regulatory safeguards. Up until now, the safeguards have worked well, although the amount of regulation is proliferating as new financial products continue to be developed. Still, there has been no German equivalent of the U.S. government's bailout of Continental Illinois in 1984, let alone a savings-and-loan–type disaster with losses in the hundreds of billions of dollars.

A good example of prudent German banking regulations is the minimum capital reserve requirements. These requirements act as a check on the amount of loans a bank can have outstanding at any one time. The German rate has always averaged around 8 percent, compared to around 4 percent in the United States and only 1 percent in Japan (although now all countries are raising their reserve levels to around 8 percent in accordance with rules laid down by the Bank for International Settlements). Because their reserve requirements were always more stringent, especially in comparison to those in Japan, German banks never figured at the top of the world rankings. Yet the quality of the German banking assets was considerably stronger, and German banks have withstood the recent worldwide banking squeeze better than most.

The knee-jerk German tendency to regulate every new development has its negative side. As Cartellieri points out, "In the old days you could list all the important bank regulations on a sheet of paper. For example, a bank should not lend over a certain percent of its assets to any one borrower, et cetera. But we bankers also knew by instinct not to do certain things. For example if you had balance sheet assets of three hundred billion deutsche marks, then you kept your off–balance sheet liabilities under, say, a hundred billion deutsche marks, or at least you didn't have five hundred billion deutsche marks in off–balance sheet liabilities. Today, there are books full of regulations dealing with items like swaps and options. By tightening the safety net around every new product, it's not just the small depositor who is protected, but the large professional as well. We have to wonder if that makes good financial sense. Also, the more you flood banks with regulation, the more you suppress the original sense of ethics."

To allow banks to deal in sophisticated and higher-risk items like swaps and options without imperiling the funds of the ordinary depositor, Cartellieri suggests a rating system for bank safety, with the bank's deposit insurance costs pegged to the ratings. The appeal of such a solution is that a bank is free to take more risks, but it must pay for the privilege. The disadvantage lies with the small banks, which, in order to keep their insurance costs down, would not be able to compete for higher-yielding business. "That is a problem," concedes Cartellieri. "But why should large banks subsidize the deposit insurance for the small?"

Banking in Euro-land

While the German bank regulators are busy piling regulations atop regulations, the Brussels bureaucrats of the EC are slowly undermining the bedrock foundations of the German banks by loosening regulations. As of 1993, the European banking market will be open to all member-country banks, making a level regulatory playing field necessary. But German bankers are not happy with some proposed EC regulations. In particular, the EC would allow banks to ascribe higher values to certain types of capital used in calculating the reserve rations, whereas the conservative Germans, of course, opt for the lower valuation method. Says Cartellieri, "We are on the one hand arguing with the EC to tighten the regulation, and on the other insisting with our own national regulators that they not put us at a disadvantage with the foreign banks should the EC rule go through."

Of all EC integration questions, none is more delicate for the banks than the creation of a central European bank, the so-called EuroFed. German banks have prospered under the tight monetary conditions imposed by the Bundesbank, which has been the de facto European central bank. Any evolution toward a central European bank, say the German bankers, should be along pragmatic —and not institutional—lines. In other words, a single European currency cannot be successfully created by fiat, but needs to evolve from the harmonization of economic and monetary policies in the member countries. Until that can be accomplished, European monetary unification should proceed at different speeds.

Already, for example, the Benelux currencies move in lockstep with the deutsche mark. In the near future, England, Italy and perhaps France could follow suit. As Cartellieri says, "Should the politicians ignore the experts, we're bound to have problems."

Banking on the Financial Markets

To argue in favor of a conservative banking ethic along German lines does not mean German banks should be treated like sacred cows. Even the bankers, particularly at the large banks, would admit that Germany needs to develop its investment banking and capital markets more. The dominance of commercial banking worked well after the war because Germany was rebuilding itself. But if Germany is to become the locomotive for Europe and play a decisive role in the development of the impoverished Eastern Europe, the parochial, private banking must become more dynamic.

The meager figures for Germany's stock market have been well publicized: only about 650 German companies are listed. Of the 650 or so companies listed, only about 120 or so are traded actively. The combined market value of all German stocks in 1990 was less than DM 600 billion, below the United States, Japan, England and Canada. Although the German bond market is the world's largest in terms of volume and securities listed, almost all the listings are for either government, financial-institution or foreign-company bonds; few German industrial bonds are listed. Walk the quiet, tree-lined streets of Frankfurt's West End, where a few skyscrapers rise above mostly three- and four-story buildings, and you are a world away from Wall Street or London's City.

If you believe Rüdiger von Rosen, the forty-eight-year-old head of the Frankfurt Stock Exchange, Germany's capital markets will be the European leaders by the end of the decade. Watching him at work, where he skips lunch, gulps coffee, bounds to the phone to speak with an enthusiasm that seems, well, un-German, you might think it possible. It's almost hard to believe he was the assistant to Karl Otto Pöhl, the totally reserved former Bundesbank president, before going to the stock market job. On the wall is a painting depicting the tearing down of the Berlin Wall. But there again you have to take von Rosen's word for it: the painting is a bit abstract.

"The competitive advantage for London because of language is gone," says von Rosen. "Business here is done more and more in English. Look at John Craven being on the management board of Deutsche Bank. That would have been unheard of a few years ago," he insists, referring to the South African–born John Craven of Morgan Grenfell, who joined the Deutsche Bank board after the 1989 merger. "My generation is Americanized." As proof, he recounts a story he told his men while he was an army officer in the mid-1960s: "I told them that the freedom of the city of Berlin was defended in Vietnam. That was stupid, but I thought it at the time."

Von Rosen also points out that in Germany today, twenty-five- to thirty-five-year-olds make up the largest group of shareholders, not in value, but at least in numbers. Demographics will work in favor of more money pouring into the German stock market. And the older Germans, who tend to be conservative, are passing on their wealth to more adventurous generations. Some estimates put the figure around DM 700 to 800 billion in the coming ten years. "This money won't just go into Porsches and Mercedeses," says von Rosen.

The real question is whether von Rosen's optimism is warranted. London as a financial center has other competitive advantages besides the English language: lower commissions, a substantial research infrastructure and well-developed futures and options markets, to name a few. And as one Frankfurt banker pointed out, "In Germany, there are only about five good analysts putting out numbers on companies, and good research for markets is like air for breathing. A firm like James Capel in London for that is second to none in Germany."

Maximilian Dietzsch-Doertenbach, forty, on the other hand, agrees with the optimistic outlook for Frankfurt. He worked in the corporate finance department at Deutsche Bank in Frankfurt before setting up his own M&A firm with a partner. He concedes that London has some advantages right now, at least for the secondary market in securities, where all you need is a computer and a telephone. But Dietzsch-Doertenbach points out that the smaller companies in Germany are not followed in London, and he sees more and more Mittelstand companies willing to tap the securities market. He also notes that as Eastern Europe grows, Germany's geographical proximity will draw business, especially in the primary market. "To structure the deals, you need the tax experts, the banks, the accountants and the lawyers, and that you cannot do over the phone."

Dietzsch-Doertenbach says he left Deutsche Bank because he wanted to provide independent advice, without worrying about commercial banking. He cites John Craven's phrase, "I have a Chinese wall going through my head," and adds that investment banking has to get out from under the banks. He points out that Germany has not always been a land of commercial banking. Back in the 1920s, German markets were using financial instruments like options and participation certificates more than is the case today. What is needed now, he says, are more alternatives to the large banks, so that Mittelstand companies and corporations do not feel as though they are being force-fed products from their house banks.

Despite the obstacles, Rüdiger von Rosen of the Frankfurt exchange is not worried. "The markets will grow anyway. Volume on German capital markets has grown by over 20 percent over the past four years, which is considerably greater than for the American markets." Germany is also in the process of consolidating its eight regional stock exchanges into one main Frankfurt central exchange, which will improve efficiency and reduce costs.

Ultimately, however, the attempt to develop German financial markets and turn Frankfurt into a financial center in the league of New York, London or Tokyo is going to force German banks to rethink how they do business. It's one thing for banks to be able to engage in every kind of financial activity, another for the banks to try to dominate every kind of financial activity. Avoiding conflicts of interest becomes impossible in the latter case, as the next chapter illustrates.

5

The Crumbling Fortress:
Takeovers in Germany

In October 1990, Eberhard von Kuenheim, the chief executive of BMW, sat on a U.S. public television panel hosted by Ted
Koppel; other guests included a number of Japanese and American
businessmen. The theme that evening: the global economy. At
one point in the discussion, von Kuenheim took the opportunity
to criticize, politely but firmly, the Japanese government's role in
foreign acquisitions of Japanese companies. "The major difference
is that in the U.S. or Germany, a foreign company does not need
to get the government's approval in order to take over a public
company," said the BMW boss. "In Japan, a foreigner cannot do
it without the government's approval."

Von Kuenheim's point about Japan is correct, but he told only half the story. German companies are quite well protected from foreign takeovers without the government's help. To suggest that German business stands on an equal footing with U.S. business in this respect is misleading. Both legally and in practice, most German public companies are protected from unfriendly take-overs by hurdles fit only for a pole vaulter. Not all the obstacles can be called downright pernicious, but add them up and it's no surprise that since the Second World War Germany has, until recently, been free from unfriendly takeovers.

Of course, the distinction between a friendly takeover and an unfriendly takeover is a fine one, rather like the distinction be-tween erotica and pornography. But the Germans know an un-friendly takeover when they see one: if an outside bidder shows up wanting to buy a company and its management and supervi-sory boards don't want it to, it's unfriendly. Color in a few gray areas, and that's what the Germans have successfully guarded against.

Assault and Battery

Two recent attempts at taking over large German companies have made the international news. One attempt came from within Ger-many, the other from outside; but both stories point up just how carefully protected German corporations have been, and how the system is finally beginning to loosen up, if only just a little. The first involved Feldmühle Nobel AG, the second Continental AG.

The Feldmühle Nobel story was not as dramatic as some American-style takeovers, but for a while at least, it did spice up the gossip columns. In early 1986 Friedrich Karl Flick sold a vari-ety of his business assets to Deutsche Bank for over DM 5 billion. The following year Deutsche Bank packaged the papermaking, chemical and heating equipment companies into one unit—called Feldmühle Nobel AG—and sold it to the public in one of the most highly subscribed initial public offerings in German history. The sale of this group of Flick's former assets alone filled Deutsche's coffers with over DM 5 billion—not a bad return. But watching from the sidelines in disbelief were two of Flick's neph-ews, Gert-Rudolf and Friedrich Christian: back in 1975 their uncle had bought out their and their sister's one-third stake in the family interests for a meager sum, about DM 300 million. Feeling gypped, the nephews wrangled with their uncle for more money. Then in 1988 they talked about taking over Feldmühle Nobel, but loose lips pushed the share price out of reach.

Meanwhile, Feldmühle's shareholders began taking defensive action in July 1988. Shareholders, led by Deutsche Bank, adopted voting rights limitations on the company's stock. No single shareholder could vote more than 5 percent of the company's outstanding share capital, regardless of the actual size of the shareholding.

Ironically, this ostensibly defensive measure helped bring about the company's loss of independence. With the possibility of a takeover supposedly diminished, the price of Feldmühle Nobel shares began to drop. Underperformance in some divisions contributed to the share price decline. By December 1988, Feldmühle Nobel's stock price had fallen below the initial offering price. The Flick nephews, who saw the value of their roughly 10 percent stake eroding, decided to take action again. With the help of the Frankfurt attorney Nicolaus Weickart and Merrill Lynch, the nephews began buying Feldmühle Nobel stock in January 1989, but not on the open market. In a few short weeks, the Flicks had quietly accumulated a 40 percent stake in the old family company.

The Flicks sold this large stake in April 1989 for a profit to the German diversified manufacturer Veba AG. The nephews reportedly turned down higher bids from other companies, claiming that Veba was the right company to reform Feldmühle Nobel, not break it up.

As it turned out, the Flicks and Weickart chose the wrong partner. Veba was not prepared to pay the price for Feldmühle Nobel's remaining outstanding shares. Instead, Veba sold its 40 percent stake to the Swedish papermaker Stora Kopparbergs Bercelags AB (and turned a profit of over DM 300 million on the transaction). Stora later raised its stake in Feldmühle Nobel to 85 percent, and sold off some of the non-papermaking divisions. The old Flick family companies had been broken up after all.

The Feldmühle Nobel affair was a clear warning that voting rights limitations were not foolproof defensive measures. That said, the passing of Feldmühle Nobel into foreign hands was, in the end, the result of a series of brokered deals, not one spectacular takeover bid. In terms of marking a turning point in German shareholder awareness, the attempted takeover of Continental AG by Pirelli SpA drew far more public attention and was of greater significance, even though Pirelli's attempt ultimately failed.

In 1990 Pirelli SpA, the big Italian tire manufacturer, began buying stock in Continental AG, with the hope of bringing about a merger of the two firms. Aware of the German aversion to hostile takeovers, the head of the Italian firm, Leopoldo Pirelli, moved cautiously, discreetly seeking the favor of Deutsche Bank's Ulrich Weiss, the head of the Continental supervisory board.

At the outset, Weiss was receptive to a possible merger. Deutsche Bank held a 5 percent stake in Conti, as the tire manufacturer is commonly known, and the bank did a lot of Conti's commercial banking business as well. Of course, if Pirelli's takeover were successful, Deutsche ran the risk of losing some of the Conti commercial banking business. On the other hand, Deutsche would build its reputation as a European player, improve its contacts in Italy and dispel the notion that it acts primarily as the protector of German industry. Besides, a successful merger could have increased the value of Deutsche's holding in Conti. Weiss told Leopoldo Pirelli to meet with Horst Urban, then the head of Conti's management board, to see if a deal were possible.

The general climate for a merger was certainly favorable enough. The tire business was in a worldwide slump. The big three—Michelin, Goodyear, Bridgestone—were suffering declining earnings, as were numbers four, Conti, and five, Pirelli. A merger, according to the Pirelli calculations, would bring economies of scale reaching DM 400 million a year, and the combined company would have a world market share of 15 percent, a tad below Bridgestone's 17 percent.

But Conti's Horst Urban knew a hostile takeover when he saw one. After all, Pirelli had begun buying Continental shares well before talks had even started. As Urban told *Der Spiegel* magazine in December 1990, "Pirelli put the gun on the table." Urban claimed he was not opposed to a merger per se, but that the terms of Pirelli's DM 2 billion reverse buyout deal were too onerous for Conti, and therefore unacceptable. The Germans would have to buy out Pirelli's shares at a premium to the market price, and to raise the money, Conti would have to issue more shares as well as borrow additional funds. Pirelli's estimates of DM 400 million in savings were greatly exaggerated. With the tire business in a slump, a merger under such terms was out of the question.

Urban was also upset that the Italians were less than forthcoming about just who exactly was buying the Conti shares: Pirelli alone or in concert with others. If the latter, then the buying was clearly more hostile. Multiple actors, aside from having a collectively deeper pocket, could also more easily get around voting rights restrictions on Conti's shares. These restrictions, the likes of which can be found at quite a few German companies, stipulate that no single shareholder can vote more than 5 percent of the company's outstanding share capital, regardless of the size of the actual shareholding.

Without waiting for Pirelli to make its exact intentions known, Urban and the Conti management dug in their heels. Ulrich Weiss was put into the embarrassing position of having to back Urban after having initially led Pirelli on. The rest of the supervisory board fell into line behind Deutsche. Naturally, the employee delegates on Conti's supervisory board were less than thrilled at the prospect of a merger, since the projected DM 400 million in savings would no doubt come from a loss of jobs.

The call went out to Conti's clients, the large German auto manufacturers, for help against the Italian offensive, and several responded. Daimler, BMW and Volkswagen, along with Deutsche Bank, Allianz and other investors, formed a shareholders' pool to buy a 25 percent stake in Conti. This stake would amount to a blocking minority, since under German corporate law, any important decisions affecting a company, such as changes in capital structure, require a 75 percent voting majority. Pirelli could still take over Conti with less than 75 percent of the shares, but the task would be much more complicated.

Thus, the early stages of the Pirelli-Conti scenario went true to form. German companies have a long tradition of helping one another out in times of trouble, and Pirelli's near-draconian merger terms made it easy for the other German companies to back Conti. Although a German management board is legally not supposed to favor one shareholder over another, the law is routinely flouted. In December 1990, Horst Urban flatly told *Der Spiegel* magazine that he would welcome a shareholder pool of German companies, and that anything to "stabilize" the Conti shares would be in the interest of the company.

But then the true-to-form scenario was upset by one Alberto Vicari, working with (some say for) the ubiquitous Frankfurt attorney Nicolaus Weickart. Vicari, who despite his Italian-sounding name is German, successfully lobbied for a special share-holders meeting in March 1991. At the meeting, which caused a big stir in German corporate circles, a majority of the shareholders present voted to do away with the voting rights limitations placed on Conti stock back in 1984.

In lobbying for the special shareholders meeting, Vicari and Weickart kept quiet as to whom they were representing. Pirelli? Other disgruntled investors in Conti shares? No matter. More and more Germans in business and financial circles were of the opinion that, aside from the merits of a Conti-Pirelli deal, the voting limitations on the Conti shares were themselves just plain wrong. Numerous articles and commentaries in the German financial press echoed this sentiment. Weickart, who is well connected to institutional investors both in Germany and abroad, has taken advantage of the growing discontent to, as he puts it, "act as a catalyst for change."

Yet in spite of this growing chorus opposed to German corporate defenses, and in spite of the March vote to eliminate voting rights restrictions on Conti shares, the voting rights limitations remained in force on Conti shares thanks to a legal technicality: the result of the March meeting was not officially entered into the corporate register.

The topsy-turvy course of the Conti affair continued long after the March meeting. Pirelli soon came back with more reasonable conditions—two seats on the Conti board and cooperation agreements between the two firms—but Urban had apparently lost interest in negotiating, claiming Conti was better equipped to go it alone. Unfortunately for him, Conti's business failed to pick up, particularly in the United States, where its General Tire subsidiary had to close down some production plants. The dismal results led Deutsche Bank, which at first had supported the idea of a merger, then balked, to change its mind yet again.

Ulrich Weiss met once more with Leopoldo Pirelli to see if a deal could be salvaged. Pirelli said maybe, but not if Urban was negotiating for Conti. Weiss and the Conti supervisory board deposed Urban—even the employee delegates dropped the obstinate manager—and replaced him with Hubertus von Grünberg, an outsider who had previously worked for ITT in the United States. Merger negotiations continued, and as late as November 1991 a deal seemed within reach. What had started out as a hostile takeover attempt and later became a cooperation agreement appeared to be on the verge of completion.

Then suddenly the talks collapsed. Pirelli's financial condition was much worse than anyone on the Conti side had imagined. Moreover, what Conti's former chief executive, Urban, had long suspected—that Pirelli was acting in concert with other buyers—turned out to be true. Pirelli had in effect guaranteed to reimburse its partners for any losses incurred on the Conti shares. The total cost to Pirelli of the aborted merger reached almost $300 million.

So another takeover attempt bit the dust, leaving another set of foreign hopefuls a little wiser and a lot poorer.

The Means Justify the Ends

How do the Germans do it? Perhaps equally important: *why* do they do it? Certainly the most obvious defense against takeovers —and the preferred German solution—is simply to remain private in the first place, a method happily employed by many of Germany's quite valuable Mittelstand companies. Of course, there are plenty of companies in Germany without that option. Let's take a look at some of the remarkably successful strategies German corporations employ to keep the takeover artists at bay.

If a company does go public, its managers will often see to it that as many shares as possible remain in friendly hands, those of people who won't necessarily sell to the highest bidder. In essence, this was the intention behind the buying of Conti shares by the German automakers. Often a company's stock is held for the most part by the original owner or by a friendly bank. Another popular solution: put the bulk of the stock into a nonprofit or other foundation. Such foundations also enable entrepreneurs to maintain their company's founding spirit after they are gone—the foundation acts as a kind of trust. Even in companies where a foundation does not hold a clear majority of the company's stock —as is the case with Thyssen—the amount of stock available to a raider can be substantially reduced.

In Germany, the nonvoting share can also be used to ward off the unfriendly. The Frankfurt exchange, in order to entice private companies to go public, lets companies list only nonvoting shares, thus allowing the controlling shares to be kept in private hands. None of the largest German corporations falls into that category, but a number of the smaller ones do.

As if the careful distribution of stock weren't enough, German corporate law can make the life of the takeover artist even more difficult. Any change in a public company's capital structure— issuing new stocks or bonds, for example—must be approved by a 75 percent majority of the voting shares. Building a blocking minority was the objective of the Conti shareholders' pool: Pirelli could have taken a 51 percent stake in Conti and replaced the supervisory—and management—boards, but a merger of the two companies through a change in capital structure, as proposed, would have been impossible if a 25 percent minority had been opposed. Of course, the holders of a 25 percent stake are probably not going to hold out indefinitely against a majority owner with other plans for the firm; it behooves no one simply to ruin the company. Still, the 25 percent stake is a significant bargaining chip. That's why, given such a minority share, the large German banks can play power broker. Recall the stakes held by Deutsche Bank—in Daimler-Benz (28 percent), Philipp Holzmann (30 percent), Karstadt (25 percent), Südzucker (20 percent)—and Commerzbank—in Karstadt (25 percent), Heidelberger Druck-maschinen (13 percent), Linde (10 percent), Salamander (10 per-cent). Even when the banks themselves don't own 25 percent of a company, their proxy voting privileges often add up to a quite effective blocking minority.

The German legal framework regarding takeover activity itself leaves much to be desired. Unlike German commercial law, which clearly spells out the rights and responsibilities of everyday business, German corporate law on takeovers is far too incomplete. Maximilian Dietzsch-Doertenbach, who left Deutsche Bank's corporate finance department to establish his own firm with a partner, explains why he opposes hostile takeovers in Germany: "In the U.S. the board has a clear objective to maximize shareholder value. There, you might almost say that a hostile takeover is one where the price is too low. In Germany there is no such guidance. There is no equivalent of the blue or yellow books in London [which spell out the conditions for making an offer, the time management has to respond, and the like]. German corporations are simply not well prepared for takeover moves."

The only current legal provision guiding managers in the event of a takeover is that they may not favor one shareholder over another. Particularly lacking is any provision spelling out what banks may do in such cases. The Conti affair is a case in point. Deutsche Bank first advised Pirelli to pursue the merger. After since-deposed Conti chief executive Horst Urban raised all sorts of objections to the terms of the proposed merger—the most important no doubt being that he would lose his job—Deutsche Bank changed its mind. Then it changed its mind again! A simple guideline requiring Deutsche Bank to choose sides early on could have eliminated such conflicts of interest and prevented Deutsche's embarrassing reversals.

The use of voting rights limitations, such as those defeated in the special Conti shareholders' meeting, is a move encouraged by some German banks—notably Deutsche Bank. Such limitations typically limit any shareholder's voting rights to, say, 5 percent of the company's share capital. Result: a single large shareholder has a tougher time exercising control. Management loves this arrangement for the obvious reason that it renders it accountable to no one but itself. When the first petrodollar wave washed onto European shores in the mid-1970s, threatening to carry off a number of industrial crown jewels in the undertow, Deutsche Bank persuaded many of the public companies in its sphere of influence to adopt such voting rights limitations.

Such limitations, however, are not necessarily airtight. Countermoves include distributing the shares among like-minded investors. And they do not apply to matters that require both a voting and a capital majority, such as changes in corporate bylaws or the company's capital structure. Furthermore, the limitations have drawn increasing fire in German business circles—they serve only to preserve the status quo—and companies are facing increasing pressure to repeal them.

Another noteworthy takeover defense is the use by some German companies of registered shares, which cannot be voted unless management agrees to register them in the acquirer's name. The shares of all German public insurance companies, for example, are typically registered. Registered shares were also at issue in a well-publicized clash of egos between German film magnate Leo Kirch and the former chief executive of the Axel Springer media company, Peter Tamm. Kirch had bought a block of registered shares that, added to shares he already owned, would have given him a 25 percent blocking minority in the Springer company. Tamm, anxious to prevent Kirch from sticking his nose into company affairs, refused for years to register the shares in Kirch's name or to give him seats on the company supervisory board. Kirch now appears to be on the verge of getting his way since Tamm was forced to step down.

Still, the use of registered shares in Germany is nowhere near the scale of that in neighboring Switzerland. There, virtually all the major public corporations are controlled exclusively by Swiss shareholders, thanks to bylaws that restrict ownership of registered shares to Swiss citizens. The major exception is, of course Nestlé SA, which caused a stir several years ago by becoming the first company to drop the nationality criterion on its registered shares.

Germany's antitakeover mentality is also bolstered by the lack of a strong group of independent company shareholders. When companies and banks hold stakes in one another and executives sit on one another's supervisory boards, the natural reflex is to stick together. A German company can underperform for years, and yet the supervisory board will continue to support the same management.

Germany also lacks several crucial sources of large amounts of independent capital. German banks have close ties to industry, and most of the large mutual funds are managed by the banks. The pension reserves are held within companies, not managed by outsiders pushing for the highest return. Compare the situation in the United States, where independent pension funds own over 25 percent of all publicly traded stock. In Germany, the only signifi-cant net owners—owners of shares not tied to the matrix of in-dustrial and bank crossholdings—are the insurance companies and foreign investors, and they are only beginning to crack the nut.

Potentially, the most "independent" of all the German insti-tutional investors is the Allianz insurance company. With DM 38 billion in revenues in 1990, Allianz is far and away the leading insurer in Europe and—since its 1990 acquisition of the Fireman's Fund insurance company—a major player in the United States. For all its independence, Allianz is tied into virtually all the major German blue-chip companies, so buying one of its shares is like buying into a mutual fund of German industry and finance.

There isn't room to name all the Allianz stakes, but they in-clude 25 percent of Munich Re, just under 23 percent of Dresdner Bank, almost 25 percent of Bayerische Hypotheken- und Wechsel-Bank, a reported 10 percent of Deutsche Bank, 36 percent of the consumer products company Beiersdorf, reportedly over 5 percent of Continental, and stakes in Thyssen, MAN, Metall-gesellschaft, Heidelberger Druckmaschinen, Mercedes, Hochtief. Those are just the most visible holdings. Allianz also has indirect holdings that give it even more control. Thus in April 1992 the German Cartel Office, claiming that Allianz indirectly controlled 47 percent of Dresdner Bank, ordered Allianz to reduce its hold-ing in the bank.

At first glance, Allianz resembles the large German banks with their vast stakes in German industry and finance. But there is a difference. Allianz holds stakes more as "pure" investments in the sense that it has no commercial banking business to protect.

So far, however, Allianz has used its power conservatively, in what might be called typical German fashion. The head of the Allianz supervisory board, Wolfgang Schieren, is on record as opposing hostile takeovers. In the Pirelli-Conti affair, for exam-ple, Friedrich Schiefer, who represented Allianz on the Conti su-pervisory board, had Allianz join the shareholder pool defending Conti. Perhaps Schiefer thought the Pirelli terms were not right, perhaps he didn't want to antagonize Deutsche Bank over this one deal. Allianz and Deutsche were already sparring over Deutsche's decision to compete with Allianz in life insurance, and an all-out battle between the two elephants could get messy.

Ultimately, the question of whether Allianz will ever sell to the highest bidder—including a hostile raider—appears to be moot. The corporate culture at the Munich-based insurer is conservative, classically blue-chip German. Said a spokeswoman for the firm, "Getting the highest price for the shares in a company is hardly the only consideration in whether to sell." Potentially, though, Allianz could cause quite a ripple throughout German business if it wanted to.

Safety in Numbers

So it may seem that, all things considered, Eberhard von Kuenheim's comments on takeovers were somewhat disingenuous. Don't all these German obstacles serve exactly the same purpose as the involvement of the Japanese government in defending Japanese companies from foreign takeovers—ensuring that German public companies remain firmly in the hands of Germans?

A call to von Kuenheim's Munich office was detoured to the head of BMW's public relations, Richard Gaul. Just for the record, BMW itself is not in the sphere of any particular bank, nor has it instituted any voting rights limitations on its stock. On the other hand, the company is quite well protected from an unfriendly takeover: a majority of its shares belong to the Quandt family. And BMW has engaged in some defensive maneuvering for the benefit of other German companies: it was involved in the German automakers' attempt to create a blocking minority of Continental stock designed to discourage Pirelli's overtures.

The amiable Gaul began with an explanation of the reasoning behind BMW's participation in the defense of Conti. BMW, he pointed out, uses three different tire suppliers—typically Conti, Pirelli and Michelin. To maintain enough competition between suppliers, BMW would have to find another if Pirelli were to take over Conti. Thus, Gaul does not view BMW's defense of Conti as particularly nationalistic at all. Of course, Gaul admits that Germany in general is not quite as open to takeovers as is the United States, even though the German government does not get involved. Nevertheless, he says, voting rights limitations and other corporate defenses are company-specific and not orchestrated by the government. Thus, he prefers to believe that Germany's attitude toward takeovers lies somewhere between that of the United States and that of Japan.

Gaul provided a telling insight into the German mentality that collectively leads to all of the various company-specific defense measures. "Here in Germany, we don't want anything like in that movie with . . . who is that actor? . . . Michael Douglas." Of course: *Wall Street,* the 1988 film for which Michael Douglas won an Academy Award for his portrayal of the unscrupulous corporate raider Gordon Gekko. "In America," continues Gaul, "a clever young man can go to a securities house and make a lot of money. In Germany he would have more luck going to the Treuhandanstalt and buying an old East German company." With these words, Gaul has gotten to the heart of what really upsets the Germans about the takeover business: the perception that there is something distinctly unhealthy about getting rich by wheeling and dealing. To the German psyche, wealth comes from production, not speculation. A better allocation of resources through the financial system may occasionally be necessary, but a wheeler-dealer must never make more money than someone who actually produces something.

What little wheeling and dealing exists in Germany is carried out almost entirely by the banks. German bankers are among the highest-paid executives in the country, but unlike takeover artists and executives of buyout firms in the United States, they don't have the opportunity to invest in deals personally. A number of smaller German firms stay active in mergers and acquisitions, but the overall volume of business is low, and the big deals generally go through the banks. Germany has no equivalent of Michael Milken and his $500 million earned in just one year, let alone a Henry Kravis who racked up an estimated $500 million fortune in a few years. If someone in Germany ever did manage to make that kind of money, the Germans would no doubt want to sit down and rewrite the laws to prevent it from happening again.

Aside from an innate German distaste for financial wheeling and dealing, the reasons for the takeover barriers are structural. German companies are vulnerable, what with their large hidden assets and heavy social expenditures on things like apprenticeship training. The last thing the Germans want is for some highly leveraged takeover artist to buy a German company and sell off the hidden assets to pay down the high debt, or scotch the expenditures on apprenticeship training to improve short-term profitability. For the barriers against takeovers to disappear, German companies would have to restructure and become more transparent. Hidden assets would need to be unlocked, and their value reflected in the firm's stock price. But not too many German businessmen are ready to take that step. The famous line uttered by Hermann Josef Abs, the longtime head of Deutsche Bank, that "hidden assets are no longer hidden if they are disclosed," still holds sway in most German business circles.

Nationalistic concerns certainly cannot be ignored when discussing takeover defenses. It was no coincidence that voting rights limitations on German shares became more popular in the mid-1970s, when the Arabs became wealthy overnight. Today the Germans—rightly or wrongly—fear a Japanese investment invasion. But the Germans are not xenophobic. Quite the opposite: their economy is far more exposed to foreign investment and imports than is that of the United States. Perhaps for that very reason, though, Germans do not want to see too many more of their prized companies fall into the hands of foreigners. In that sense Germans are no different from Americans, who complain every time a Japanese company buys another New York City skyscraper or Hollywood studio. In Germany, foreigners are welcome as long as they do not come riding into town trailing a wagonload of borrowed cash and looking to make a quick deutsche mark.

Yet for all the justifications the Germans can muster in defense of their barriers against takeovers, they smack of a double standard, since, well protected as they are, German companies have amply demonstrated their own willingness to engage in hostile takeovers abroad. The acquisition of Britain's Plessey Plc. in 1990 by Siemens and Britain's General Electric was about as "hostile" as an acquisition can get. Both Plessey's management and board of directors opposed the takeover, and before the dust settled, the British government stepped in to ensure that the company's sensitive military operations would remain with British firms.

Furthermore, the German banks, so protective of companies at home, do not hesitate to fall in with predators abroad. Through its acquisition of Morgan Grenfell, for example, Deutsche Bank is now up to its neck in hostile takeovers outside Germany. Thus the pressure is clearly on the German banks to create a more level playing field at home.

Cracks and Fissures

The Feldmühle and Conti cases have shown that a few cracks are beginning to appear in the walls of Fortress Deutschland. Indeed, a growing number of people in German business circles realize that German companies must open up to shareholders; if Germany really wants to take part in a frictionless European common market, the country's anachronistic business climate must change. One command post for shareholder interests can be found at the Deutsche Schutzvereinigung für Wertpapierbesitz (DSW) in Düsseldorf. Nominally headed by Otto Graf Lambsdorff, better known as the leader of Germany's centrist Free Democratic Party, the DSW is really an association of corporate lawyers and free market activists trying to promote shareholder rights on behalf of the association's members—individual shareholders in German companies or foreign corporations who want their voices heard in Germany. You do not find DSW activists handcuffing themselves to fences or unfurling slogan-filled banners from the roofs of buildings; rather, they do their best to draw attention to company managements that are hostile to shareholders—while freely praising the good ones.

The DSW takes positions on a variety of issues. Particularly loathsome in its eyes: voting rights limitations and the issuance of nonvoting shares. Every year the DSW commends those companies providing the most complete disclosure in their annual reports, a list that recently included Karstadt, Bayer, RWE and VEW.

The real trench work takes place in shareholder meetings and, in a few cases, the courtroom. The DSW will typically send a representative to a shareholders' meeting on behalf of a shareholder who cannot attend and wants his vote counted or a particular question answered. In 1990 the DSW was present at over four hundred such meetings, not bad considering that only 650 companies are publicly listed in Germany. As Peter Staab, a lawyer with the DSW, points out, a lot goes on in these meetings that might not filter out into the company's annual report or the financial press. He cites a recent example in which a British investor wanted to know how much real estate a certain company held in Berlin. Staab raised the question at a shareholders' meeting and discovered that, lo and behold, the company owned lots of land in central Berlin. The Brit was confounded. Why had he not read about this hidden asset anywhere? The answer, as Staab points out, is that the company simply never bothered to let anyone know.

The lack of foreign shareholder representation at the meetings in Germany is indeed a problem. "It makes German management boards arrogant toward foreign shareholders," says Staab. The sooner foreigners start making their voices heard, either in person or through an agent like the DSW, the faster the insular world of the German management board can be shaken up.

It would appear that the prevailing winds in German business are beginning to shift, coming around to more shareholder activism—if slowly. Nicolaus Weickart and Alberto Vicari, flush from their initial victory at Continental, have taken their campaign to the doors of Veba AG, where they want to do away with a corporate holding structure that they say minimizes shareholder value.

Veba's business activities cover oil, chemicals, trading and electric power, but the share price of the diversified company has lagged behind the German market index in recent years. According to Weickart and Vicari, Veba would better serve shareholders by taking its various divisions public as independent companies and then holding controlling stakes in the newly created companies. Alberto Vicari even warned Veba's management at the 1991 shareholder meeting, in so many words, "if you do not create [shareholder] value, others will do it."

Veba's management is resolutely opposed to the proposal, saying the benefits would only go to the German tax authorities, and that the company's diversification is necessary to help weather cyclical downturns in any one sector. Stay tuned.

And then there is Sabo Group. This small public company—sales were DM 125 million in 1990—manufactures lawn mowers and was taken public by Deutsche Bank in 1987. The shares first flashed on brokers' screens with a 10 percent voting rights limitation already built in, and only by a greater than 75 percent majority vote could Sabo shareholders do away with the limitation. But in March 1991, while most of the business press was busy following the Pirelli–Conti affair, Sabo shareholders—led by three insurance companies—ignored management's recommendations and by an 80 percent majority voted to do away with the limitations. A few months later a controlling stake in the company was sold to the American firm John Deere.

How did Sabo's management adapt to the loss of independence? Quite well, in fact. Hans Reumann, a Sabo executive, says that the Americans stuck with the same management and did not try to disrupt the company. "The acquisition has worked very well for both firms, and our businesses complement one another very well." Would Sabo management have considered teaming up with John Deere had the shareholders not taken matters into their own hands? "Probably not. It would have been too early," says Reumann. "But with hindsight, we see only advantages."

PART TWO

THE LIFE OF
GERMAN BUSINESS

"What makes the character or corporate culture of a company is the
people and the structure. If people know your system from the
bottom up, they know your thinking process.
It is a bit like mother's milk."

—UWE THOMSEN

6
_____

The Fine Art of Backscratching:
The German Social Market

What would the United States be like if management and labor got along, jobs—usually held by highly skilled workers trained by the corporations—were a primary concern, corporations had the breathing room to plan years ahead, everyone had six weeks of paid vacation, productivity was high and unemployment was low?

While it has its problems, Germany fits that description pretty well. How do the Germans do it? What's the secret? Well, there's no secret, no hocus-pocus. German business proceeds—and succeeds—in part by maintaining a degree of social commitment unheard of in the United States.

Employment as a Greater Good

The term "social market economy," so frequently applied to Germany's system of capitalism, is all too often taken as a synonym for government intervention in an otherwise private, capitalist economy. Wrong.

The source of German capitalism's heightened social awareness lies as much in private companies as in any government regulation. The close ties between German business and the larger society have their roots in the history and continuing importance of the Mittelstand, the enormous and still powerful group of small and medium-size businesses whose source of strength remains the local community. Perhaps equally important, big business in Germany plays a strong supporting role in the larger German society as well. When it comes to meeting the social needs of the country, German companies frequently step forward and take responsibility before the government feels it necessary to interfere.

Nowhere is the social philosophy of German business more visible than in the case of employment. German business is characterized in large part by consensus—not conflict—between corporate management and labor unions: together, they set national employment policy. Both parties have consistently—and perhaps surprisingly—found their individual interests to be closely linked. Even though a variety of pressures—highly competitive markets, reunification, the plight of the guest worker, the opening of the Eastern European markets—is currently bearing down on the social contract of German business, that contract remains fully in effect.

The German social contract leaves plenty of room for the individual. German workers take pride in their companies and tend to be very loyal to them, but they also have a life outside the company. Compare Japan, where the life of the company takes precedence over that of the individual. Germans do not necessarily socialize after hours with their colleagues from work, nor do they wind up in a company cemetery at the end of their years.

For the owners and bosses of German companies, the social contract implies a right to maximize profits, but also a responsibility to the employees and the community in which they live and work. Rights and responsibilities go together, and a German company has a responsibility to more than just its owner. The contrast with the American business philosophy is noticeable.

In the United States, company owners or shareholders are king, and the truest measure of success at a U.S. company is the bottom line, often at the expense of all else. All too often, owners and shareholders want the biggest bang for their buck. Such a view is not necessarily antisocial; we like to assume that profits are reinvested, creating more jobs. But American business tends to look at jobs as factors of production, not people. Consider the annual rankings of leading corporations in the U.S. financial press. The yardsticks are typically sales, profits, assets and market value; the number of jobs a company provides is, if anything, an afterthought listed only as an indication of productivity. The fewer the jobs, the better.

To the Germans, the number of jobs a company provides is as important as sales volume and profitability. When the *Frankfurter Allgemeine Zeitung,* one of Germany's leading financial newspapers, does its yearly rankings of German companies, the yardsticks used are sales, profits and total number of jobs. The same paper is quite capable of running an article with a headline like "Siemens provided 5,000 more jobs this year than last." In the United States, no major financial publication would run such a headline; only in the regional press, where it seems jobs still count for something, might such an item be considered newsworthy.

Concern for employees in German business is even reflected in the language. An employee in German is a *Mitarbeiter*—a co-worker. Negotiations between labor and management take place between the *Sozialpartner*[s]. Such thinking is not just a linguistic quirk. Large companies issue, in addition to their usual annual reports, a "social report" dealing with such topics as the number of jobs, improvements in job quality, productivity issues and so forth. Whether shareholders outside the company really bother to read such reports could be debated, but the effort to provide more insight into working conditions—and not just a few glossy photos of smiling employees on the front cover of the annual report —is an indication that someone cares.

Germans do not believe that society has a greater interest in how a company is run than the owner has, but they do feel strongly that an owner's interests are also the interests of society.

The takeover frenzy in the United States during the 1980s, for example, which was driven by leveraged buyout firms and the brokerage industry, was perceived almost unanimously in German business circles as entirely counterproductive, skewed toward the enrichment of a select group of individuals and certainly not to everyone's advantage. Because jobs are virtually sacred in Germany, Germans zealously guard against the fast-money crowd laying its hands on German companies. The thought of a corporate raider eliminating an entire division overnight to save money and meet outrageous interest payments horrifies not only German workers and their unions—no big surprise—but the uppermost echelons of German management as well.

When a German company falls on hard times, a great deal of unspoken pressure can be exerted for a larger, more successful German company or bank to come to the rescue and preserve the jobs. As Bernd Stecher, head of external relations at Siemens, explains, "Employment is a public issue, and private German companies identify with it." Such was the case in 1989, when Siemens came to the rescue of the troubled Nixdorf computer manufacturer four years after founder Heinz Nixdorf died. One of Siemens' stated goals was to preserve all 51,000 Nixdorf jobs. Alas, it was not to be. Integrating Nixdorf's workstations with Siemens' other lines of computers turned out to be thornier than expected, and in 1991 Siemens Nixdorf trimmed 3,000 workers from its payrolls. A similar scenario may be under way with Deutsche Bank, which in 1990 bought up the retail banking operations of the defunct East German state bank. The stated goal was to maintain jobs for every one of the 8,300 workers. Deutsche Bank, with its deep pockets, may better be able to afford the luxury of bringing the business to the jobs. In the meantime the public relations value doesn't hurt.

A Private Affair

The ties that bind German companies to their communities go far beyond creating and sustaining employment. In conjunction with state-sponsored vocational schools, German companies voluntarily pay upwards of 15 percent of their net incomes to provide apprenticeship training to young workers aged fifteen and up. An owner interested in short-term profits could easily slash the apprenticeship program, boosting net income immediately, but the education and skill of the people in the community would be directly and adversely affected. The German businessman implicitly understands the effect such a loss of training would have on the productivity of his workers. Thus self-interest and the needs of the community meet, to the benefit of all.

On another social front, numerous corporations, including some of Germany's largest—Bosch, Krupp, Thyssen, Bertelsmann—have nonprofit foundations as major shareholders. The purpose of these foundations, and their statutes, vary greatly, but they typically use company dividends to support a wide range of research and cultural activities. The Robert Bosch foundation, for example, owns some 90 percent of the company's stock and uses company dividends to promote hospitals and medical research, among other goals. Naturally, such foundations, if not direct advertising arms of the companies, can still enhance the public image of the firm. The Bertelsmann foundation awards a fairly well publicized prize of DM 300,000 every year to a person who demonstrates creativity and innovation in business.

The German foundations thus differ from those in the United States, where laws were passed in the 1970s to prohibit direct links between nonprofit foundations and for-profit companies. The fear was that wealthy entrepreneurs would use the foundations as an end run around the tax code to further their company or personal interests. Today, the Ford Foundation, created by Henry Ford in 1936, shares only its name with the Ford Motor Company (the foundation started going its own way beginning in the 1950s). The Ford Foundation must raise money privately. The Germans, on the other hand, allow companies to help finance foundation activities, and the finance ministry supervises the foundations. If a company is blatantly using the foundation to further its for-profit activities—say, a foundation brochure carries company advertising—the tax authorities assess a penalty. Also, every thirty years, German foundations have to pay a kind of presumed "inheritance tax," as though the foundation had been passed on to the next generation. In the end, nonprofit foundations that enjoy tax advantages cannot be used by entrepreneurs or corporations to circumvent the tax laws; the system is simply too strict.

And the environment? German companies, which are in the forefront of recycling technology, can claim as good an environmental record as companies anywhere in the world. The reason has less to do with the widely hyped Green party than with the realities of living in a highly industrialized, densely populated country. Several communities along its banks depend on the industrial waterway, the Rhine, for drinking water—at least indirectly. Water from the Rhine is purified and then pumped into the ground, where it is further cleansed before becoming part of the underground water table and fit to drink. The need to recycle in Germany is present everywhere and is not limited to Rhine River water or beer bottles. Without vast forests like those in Scandinavia or Canada to draw from, German papermakers such as Haindl use high-technology de-inking equipment to increase the content of recycled paper in their newsprint. Germans may love their automobiles, but they are rapidly running out of room in which to dump them. Mercedes-Benz, BMW and Volkswagen are working on ways to build a 100 percent recyclable car.

While the Green party and local opposition groups feeding off a "not in my backyard" syndrome have a strong influence, they are by no means fatal for business. The more realistic—and influential—wing of the Green party knows how to compromise. And concern for the environment runs deep in German business regardless of party affiliation. Erivan Haub, who owns the Tengelmann chain of supermarkets in Germany (and a majority stake in A&P in the United States), was quick to ban phosphate detergents from his stores as well as fish from Iceland, which ignores international appeals to stop whale hunting. Yet Haub is no left-winger: he took out full-page ads in German papers thanking the United States for coming to the rescue of Kuwait. Even the ruling German conservative coalition can demonstrate a more-than-symbolic concern for the environment: it recently passed a law that requires every company to name a manager responsible for ensuring compliance with environmental laws.

Wriggling Free

Still, the German businessman—like his counterparts everywhere —can sometimes be pushed too far. There are limits to what social causes German corporations are willing to take on. The German social market is not entirely social. Companies must remain competitive, and sometimes that means finding ways to cut costs.

The *Gewerbesteuer,* a tax companies must pay to the communities in which they operate in addition to the regular corporate income tax, is the object of considerable criticism in corporate circles. Based on a company's assets and not its income, the *Gewerbesteuer* may represent as much as 20 percent of the company's total tax bill; the fact that a company can lose money in a given year and still have to pay seems unfair to many. Even more galling, perhaps, is the fact that the tax can vary widely from town to town. During the rapid-expansion years of the 1960s, the Robert Bosch company, renowned for its dedication to its employees, shifted its headquarters from the city of Stuttgart to Gerlingen, just over the town line: more space was available, as was a much lower *Gewerbesteuer*. Still, the tax remains in place because communities depend so heavily on it: in some cases it can mean more than 50 percent of a town's annual tax revenue.

And German companies must help provide health insurance for the general population, since most Germans—working or retired—are insured by a regional, paragovernmental institution, the Allgemeine Ortskrankenkasse. Funding is provided by matching contributions from employers and employees, usually around 6 percent of a worker's salary. In an attempt to cut costs, a number of the larger corporations such as Audi have decided to create their own health insurance funds, but the idea has by no means met with universal approval. One major concern: private company funds don't actually lower costs through better management. Rather, these companies place the youngest, ablest, lowest-risk people into their company fund, leaving the regional fund with a smaller pool of contributors and a more elderly, higher-risk membership. Some opponents want to apply pressure on those companies setting up their own funds to compensate the standard community funds for the difference. Either way, like it

or not, German companies would continue to support health insurance for the population as a whole.

If German companies occasionally try to evade certain generally accepted social obligations, such as community health insurance or a particularly high local tax, it's because Germany is
not some autarchic social wonderland. The German economy is
for the most part wide open to foreign imports, and invisible
obstacles to foreign competition are nowhere near as complex as
they are in, say, Japan. German companies do a lot for German
society, but they must also remain competitive.

Few German companies are pampered by their government.
The hard-hit coal and shipbuilding industries were subsidized for
several years beginning in the 1970s, but lately the German government has signaled its intention to reduce these subsidies. Government help for the telecommunications industry has also been
on the way down as the government looks to restructure the
Bundespost, the state-owned mail and telecommunications company, in the coming years. The state-owned airline, Lufthansa, is
another oft-mentioned candidate for privatization in the future.

United We Stand

German business is proof that it is entirely possible to compete in
a tough, open market and at the same time provide strong support
for the society at large. Indeed, a bit of social responsibility in the
corporate suite can go a long way toward earning the respect of
the men and women on the factory floor. The social conflict that
characterizes many European countries—and to some extent the
United States—is far less pronounced in Germany. Thus it's not
all that surprising that during the 1980s Germany outpaced the
United States in overall productivity gains—gross domestic production divided by the number of workers—even as Germans
managed to work fewer hours and take more vacations.

Compared to Americans and Japanese, Germans do indeed
have reduced hours. The average German workweek consists of
37 hours, compared to around 41 in the United States and over 60
in Japan. Germans have six weeks of vacation, all of which they
take. Furthermore, in Germany the so-called second wage—noncash benefits paid by employers—has climbed steadily since the

early days of the economic miracle; now they are equal to over 80 percent of a worker's take-home pay. Government-mandated benefits such as social security and accident insurance add up to about one third of take-home pay. In addition, German workers have received many benefits via management-labor wage negotiations: not only do they get a Christmas bonus, they also get an extra month's pay when they take their annual six-week vacation.

How do the Germans do it? "It's no secret," says Jörg Barczynski, head of press relations for the IG Metall union. "About twenty or thirty years ago unions in America had to make a choice between fighting for higher wages or for fewer hours and more benefits. They chose the former." Barczynski thus rejects the notion that benefits are "added" to a German worker's wages, and suggests instead that these benefits are "substituted." Nor does he feel that these noncash labor costs hinder greater employment: "If they [management] need people, they will hire." Also, what counts in the eyes of the German unions is stable jobs, not temporary ones: "We would prefer to see fewer hirings in the [economic] upswing if the jobs are just going to disappear in the downswing."

In fact, it is fair to say that the good relationship that exists between management and the unions is in many ways responsible not only for Germany's smoothly running social market but also for the miracle of German productivity itself. When Werner Otto pointed out in his book that the unions had enabled entrepreneurs like himself to raise the standard of living for his employees without losing a competitive advantage, he spoke for many in German management. There will always be entrepreneurs and managers who begrudge anything a union does, but a majority of German entrepreneurs and top managers would concur that the unions have played a positive, stabilizing role in labor-management relations.

IG Metall, Barczynski's reputedly feisty metalworkers' union, is typical. With more than 3.5 million members in the steel, automobile and other industries, IG (*Industriegewerkschaft,* or "union") Metall is the largest, most powerful union in Germany. (The umbrella organization for the many German unions, the Deutscher Gewerkschaftsbund, does not take part in wage negotiations.)

IG Metall sees itself as a fighter's union, one which under no circumstances, as union boss Franz Steinkühler puts it, will become the junior partner to capital interests. But capital interests do not always coincide with those of management, and German unions like IG Metall know how to work with German management. Says Barczynski, "We want investment and management wants investment, while capital interests [shareholders and owners] want dividends. We do not press our wage demands to the point where management has no money left to reinvest. The most secure jobs are those in a modern factory." In other words, one secret of Germany's harmonious management-labor relations is that strong unions and strong management form an effective alliance against capital interests in the three-way tug-of-war over profits. By contrast, managers in the United States are less entrenched and tend to ally with capital interests, with the result that management-labor relationships tend to be adversarial. Barczynski's view of management-labor relations in the United States is dim: "Each side seems to think the other is trying to pull a fast one. With such an atmosphere we could not work here."

Barczynski also attributes Germany's good labor-management relations to the recognition by employers of the value of human capital and the recognition by unions of the cost of strikes to all concerned. "The last major strike in the metal industry was in 1984 over reduced hours," says Barczynski. "It lasted seven weeks, cost us over DM 500 million and cost management a lot more."

Barczynski's response to the charge that German competitiveness is hurt by the reduced hours? Industry, he believes, was already kicking and screaming when the number of hours was brought down from 40 to 38.5 and to 37, yet in the same period one export record after another was surpassed. Two hundred thousand jobs have been created in the metal industry over the last several years, he says, although there is some disagreement between management and unions as to whether the reduced hours or the business boom of the 1980s contributed more to their creation.

Figures provided to *Forbes* magazine in July 1991 by Ford Europe suggest a similar conclusion: even though the average hourly labor cost in Germany came to $23.90 compared to $15.60 in

Britain, the number of direct and indirect labor-hours required to build a car in Germany was only 31, compared to 50 in Britain. Do the math, and it's clear that "Made in Germany" need not cost more. (The one hitch in the equation is that, according to Ford, only 22 total labor-hours go into producing a Japanese car. If the Japanese were to begin manufacturing, not just assembling, cars in Britain, they would undercut the German competition.)

Even though IG Metall and other German unions drive a hard bargain on hourly reductions, they do not waste management's time with the sort of political agenda pushed by many unions in other European countries. In France and Italy, for example, the leading unions have direct ties to their country's communist parties. In Britain, it wasn't until Margaret Thatcher came along that the unions, closely tied to the Labour Party, were broken. Germany has never had that problem: the Nazis had no use for unions in their state-controlled economy, and after the war the Americans used their influence to help create a strong union movement that succeeded in remaining independent of political parties.

The apolitical and yet essentially progressive role of German unions is a lesson for Germany's European neighbors. Daniel Goeudevert, the number-two executive at Volkswagen, is a Frenchman by birth who worked for Citroën and Ford Germany before going to VW. He explained to a French television interviewer that when dealing with unions in Germany, agreeing to the union's demands or at least showing a willingness to negotiate more than makes up for higher costs through increased productivity and fewer strikes.

Getting other unions in Europe to follow the German lead is no easy task, however. Ongoing attempts to coordinate the various union policies through direct ties and through European organizations based in Brussels have met with little success. As Barczynski points out, "We don't like communists. Free unions and communism do not go together. Thus, we have no ties with the CGT in France [the largest French union]. They are not in the European Federation of Metalworkers [a Brussels-based umbrella group]. The Italian communists are in, but that's another story," says Barczynski with a smile, referring to the less-than-dogmatic discipline of the Italian communists.

German unions are also enthusiastic supporters of codetermination, whereby labor representatives have powers within the company through employee councils as well as power on company supervisory boards, where they sit next to outside directors. "For a long time," says Barczynski, "the unions in other countries said that codetermination is crazy, akin to fraternizing with the enemy. The British unions, for example, felt that labor was the exploited class, and management and capital was the exploiting class. Only recently have the British unions come around somewhat.

"We have another problem," continues Barczynski, "in that management throughout Europe all speaks English and managers understand one another. We try to organize the workers—one speaks Spanish, the other French or German. I cannot go to Greece and explain there that a thirty-five-hour workweek is important and higher wages are less important. Only a Greek can do that. It took five or six years to convince other European unions to get behind hourly reductions. The Italians wanted flexible hours, because all Italians have two jobs, one declared and one moonlighting, and it's easier to do that with flexible hours. Now, however, most unions are working at reducing the number of hours. In England and in Belgium the number of hours is coming down."

Three's a Crowd

No discussion of social conditions for workers in Germany can overlook the fate of the so-called guest workers. Beginning with Italians in the 1960s and continuing with the Portuguese, Greeks, Yugoslavs and especially Turks in the early 1970s, immigrant labor in Germany reached a total of 4.5 million. Like the Algerians in France and the Indians and Pakistanis in Britain, immigrant labor in Germany did many of the jobs that no Germans wanted. The major difference is that the German guest workers were never ex–colonial subjects like the Algerians or Indians, and Germans never felt any obligation to make citizenship readily available to these workers. In fact, as unemployment in Germany reached high levels in the early 1980s, the German government even offered guest workers a small amount of cash and a one-way train ticket home. This pragmatic solution, criticized by some as cal-

lous, was nevertheless accepted by a good number of guest workers, who did not care about German citizenship anyway.

Indeed, many of the guest workers do not want German citizenship. Their goal is to work in Germany for several years and
save as much money as possible for the family back home before
they go there themselves and retire. It is still not uncommon for
three or four male Turks or Yugoslavs to save money by piling
into a single studio apartment, where the living conditions tend
to resemble—at least in the eyes of the squeaky-clean Germans—
a pigsty.

The bad reputation which accompanies many of the guest
workers unfortunately spills over onto those who would gladly
adopt a more German way of life. For these wanna-be Germans,
the discrimination in everyday life, combined with the vagaries of
the German naturalization law, is a bitter slap in the face. A Turk
could live, work and pay taxes in Germany for twenty years and
still not get citizenship, while a Russian from the Volga whose
Germanic ancestry, as one politician sarcastically put it, consisted
of once owning a German shepherd, could be naturalized almost
immediately.

For many of the guest workers in Germany, especially the
Turks with their alien Moslem culture, life is a contrast in discrimination. In the workplace there is virtually none—the guest
worker receives the same pay and the same voting privileges for
workers' councils and other company elections. In private life,
however, finding housing or schools for children, or having a
voice in community affairs, can be a major hurdle. Then there are
the occasional neo-Nazis or other poor white trash who, with no
one else to pick on, turn their wrath on the Turks, subjecting
them to verbal and physical harassment.

Within the companies, the unions have done a good job defending the rights of the guest workers. IG Metall's Barczynski
points to the widespread representation of guest workers on
workers' councils and speaks with pride of the 120 workers' councils in the metal industry whose presidents are guest workers:
"They were elected by Germans and non-Germans alike." Outside the companies, however, the unions have a more difficult
time. Both the unions and the opposition Social Democratic party
(SPD) want to give guest workers more of a say in local govern-

ment: "If you live in Frankfurt for twenty years, you ought to have a say in the water prices," says Barczynski. The unions and the SPD would also like to make the naturalization process for longtime guest workers easier. The ruling conservative coalition, however, opposes both measures. As for giving the guest workers a vote in general German elections, "Nobody wants that," says Barczynski.

The German social market has been a source of wonder for many admirers outside Germany. And why not? Who wouldn't welcome increased production, exports and productivity accompanied by a rising standard of living? What remains to be seen, however, is how long the Germans can keep it up.

Already reunification with eastern Germany has provided a major challenge for the German social contract. Much was written in the first year after reunification about the gulf that still divided the two Germanies. West Germans felt the need to constantly remind their eastern brethren that the spoils of capitalism come only to those who have toiled for a few years first, while the former East Germans resented being treated like second-class citizens. Nevertheless, much of what makes the German social contract so enviable was very evident to those who bothered to notice. Countless German companies leaped over the gulf before they knew if there was solid footing on the other side by buying dilapidated East German companies and saving whatever jobs they could. Private citizens gave freely of their time to help train and educate their compatriots in the East. Numerous television and radio talk shows aired in prime time served as forums for leading businessmen, government ministers and citizens on both sides to assess progress and figure out new directions. Mere numbers and statistics do not begin to tell the whole story.

Still, doubters can rightfully wonder if the Germans are not extending the country's social benefits eastward too hastily. IG Metall, for instance, drove a hard bargain to have eastern wage levels meet those in the West by 1994. But aren't the unions putting the cart before the horse, especially if productivity gains don't match the increase in wages? Barczynski doesn't think so. "The problem is two economies in the East functioning side by side. Where you have western investment in the East, you have the highest productivity, since the machines are brand new. Volkswagen is building a factory near Zwickau with brand-new machines and even greater productivity than in Wolfsburg [the site of the main VW plant in the West]. The investments also benefit from special government subsidies [such as tax breaks]. Why should we give Mr. Hahn [chief executive of VW] the added advantage of still lower wages than in the West?

"Then we have another problem, most evident in the services sector, but also in others. The Berlin subway operator who drives the train from Bahnhof Zoo [in the West] to Berlin Hauptbahnhof [in the East] earns DM 3,500 per month, while the other guy, who drives the same train in the other direction, gets only DM 1,500 per month for the same work. How long can this discrepancy be maintained? Some argue that the cost of living in the East is cheaper. But already food costs the same. Only apartment rents are cheaper, and these rents need to go up if the building owners are ever going to renovate the rotted-out buildings.

"The biggest problem is with the companies still held by the Treuhandanstalt [the agency charged with privatizing East German businesses], which are not attracting investors and cannot afford the higher wages. We feel that in those cases the government has to subsidize the wages, at least for a short while. The government wanted instant reunification for political reasons. We would have preferred to see two currency zones for a while to protect the eastern economy. The higher wages in troubled eastern companies are a cost of the political reunification. The taxpayers will have to pay. We are the taxpayers. It is absurd to think that West Germany can afford reunification for free." True, perhaps, but expecting the government to pay for reunification in the form of wage and benefit subsidies is a far cry from the spirit of the German social market. As it now stands, private industry will have to bear the brunt of those costs.

With the "velvet" revolutions of Eastern Europe, an additional problem has arrived for the unions. At the same time as the unions are desperately trying to raise the standard of living for the ex–East Germans, they must also contend with a massive influx of illegal workers from Poland, Czechoslovakia and other points east. As many as 40,000 illegal workers entered Germany in the

first six months of 1991 alone, and the German border with Poland and Czechoslovakia is beginning to resemble the United
States' Mexican border. The government has stepped up border
patrols, but the Germans would much rather see improved economic conditions in Eastern Europe than another militarized
zone.

7

The First Steps in Business: The Corporate Apprenticeship

Every year, Anke Weber gets together with her fellow schoolteachers in Weinheim, a small town just north of Heidelberg, to determine the future of her nine- or ten-year-old elementary school pupils. At this tender age, the children first encounter the dual system of German education. The pupils with better grades are put onto the scholastic track, while the remainder attend either a *Realschule* or a *Hauptschule,* where the pace is slower and vocational training is the goal (the pace at the *Hauptschule* is the slowest).

This type of preadolescent preselection is not as draconian as it sounds. Weber says that out of a class of thirty students there are only one or two borderline cases. Besides, the students can always switch tracks. They may lose a year in the process, but switching is not uncommon and there's no stigma attached. German universities also have an admissions route for kids on the vocational track.

One advantage of the German dual system is that it does away with the fiction that every child wants, or needs, an education devoted entirely to the liberal arts. Another is that it provides German business with its greatest asset: the apprentice. Plenty of German youths are content to find a vocation—mechanic, chemical lab technician and the like. For them, German business offers a vast array of apprenticeships, which students enter around the age of fifteen. They spend three or four days a week learning at the company, and another day and a half at a state-run vocational school. In this fashion, German companies also assure themselves a steady supply of skilled labor.

Skills That Matter

German business excels in the quality of its work force. Here we're not talking so much about the chief executives and top managers. They are often intelligent, but no more so than the heads of corporations in the United States, Japan or other countries. Where Germans have an edge is in the skill of the factory workers, secretaries and so forth. Like their bosses, these employers come to do their jobs well through extensive apprenticeship programs.

The concept of apprenticeship means little to the American business community. Corporations here rarely open their doors to apprentices; they take on an occasional college student as an intern for a summer or a few hours a week, during which period the person hangs around the office, drinks coffee, reads the paper and adjusts to wearing a tie or stockings. German apprenticeship doesn't compare. Job training is available for teenagers in a wide variety of professions, both blue collar and white collar, and successful completion is contingent upon passing numerous exams. It's real training for a real job, far more exhaustive and demanding. Ironically, when it comes to thinking of ways of making U.S. companies more competitive in world markets, corporations here often pay lip service to the importance of training youth, but there are always enough experts who would prefer to focus on "important" issues like trade restrictions, strategic mergers, and the latest management techniques. In Germany, the lowly teenage apprentice, or *Lehrling,* is not an issue. He or she is a cherished resource, worth a hundred management theories.

Moreover, the proven success of apprenticeship training for blue-collar workers has led the Germans to offer apprenticeships for all sorts of white-collar professions as well; many of those in the higher echelons in corporate Germany today took part in an apprenticeship program early on in their careers. The apprentice-ship is by no means a prerequisite for success at the top: plenty of German chief executives have succeeded without one. Neverthe-less, the apprenticeship instills a common bond that lasts with an employee as he or she rises through the ranks. It's a bit like a corporate boot camp.

The German corporation's commitment to apprenticeships is reflected in the money ponied up for training employees—in some cases the equivalent of a Harvard education. German employers, from Volkswagen to small Bavarian brewers, the chemical com-pany Hoechst to small engineering firms, take responsibility for their new employees in a way that American employers never have. German corporations make this educational commitment not because they have the money to pay for a few years of down-time and classwork on the job—they weren't always riding the wave of a booming economy. Training is a German tradition. Over the centuries, a two- or three-year apprenticeship for new employees has been incorporated into the German way of school-ing and business.

German managers sink money into teaching and training in the same way an American corporation might fund new-product development. And, in turn, their employees—and their products —benefit. These years of corporate training make an indelible mark on the German employee and his business practice. All recall their memorable first step onto the corporate ladder. In Germany the apprenticeship is an entire system, not just an ad hoc govern-ment jobs program. Virtually every German is assured a foot in the door for job training and in most cases a job upon completion. The closest equivalent in the United States is the army, where—

if you believe the ads—you can be all you can be. But the U.S. Army doesn't provide nearly the breadth of job training, and as the recent Persian Gulf crisis illustrates, the U.S. Army's primary mission is occasionally military, not economic.

A Throwback for the Future

The German apprenticeship system has been in existence since the fourteenth century. Originally, guilds were created for professions like baker, woodworker and shoemaker in order to protect so-called mutual interests. Only a *Meister,* or master, was qualified to take on apprentices, and in order to become a master, you had to pass an apprenticeship and serve a long stint as a tradesman. In fact, these guilds were overbearing cartels, setting prices and limiting entry into the profession. Even if you had the skills to be a shoemaker, you were out of luck unless you worked through the guild. Also, in those days the terms of an apprenticeship were reversed. You, or more likely your parents, had to pay the master tradesman to take you on. An apprenticeship might last five years, a stint as a journeyman another ten. Only then could you be certified by the guild as a master.

This guild system functioned with relatively few changes up until the rise of the industrial revolution in Germany at the end of the nineteenth century. Then came the crucial test. The use of machines supposedly reduced human labor to perfunctory, rote tasks. Why spend time and money teaching a laborer how an engine works if all he has to do is fasten bolts all day? In most European countries, the training of skilled labor was phased out. But in Germany, industry simply took over the role of the old guilds and spent its own money to train workers.

There's no simple explanation for why German industrialists took on the job-training role when many of their European counterparts did not. To some extent, the strong socialist school of thought flourishing in German academic circles at the time spilled over to conservatives and capitalists. Even Otto von Bismarck, the iron-fisted ruler who created modern Germany and handily defeated the French in 1870, stood behind social legislation in the 1880s. While those laws never addressed apprenticeships (they concerned insurance for accidents, retirement and sickness), many private employers saw to it that the apprenticeship system continued.

Early in the twentieth century, German industrialists voluntarily began coordinating apprenticeship programs. The result was a more fluid job market. A machine tool company in the Ruhr could hire a recently graduated apprentice machinist from, say, Bavaria and know what skills he had learned.

The voluntary approach lasted until 1969, when the federal government, looking to ensure that apprentices weren't "exploited" by private companies as cheap labor, passed the *Berufsbildungsgesetz*. This law authorized local chambers of commerce and industry to approve a company's right to train apprentices. The law also gave the federal government ultimate authority over the terms of contract between an employer and an apprentice, the remuneration, the examination system and other related matters. Yet for all the government's involvement, the impetus behind apprenticeships has always come from the companies doing the training. That was also the case in East Germany, where the apprenticeship system was maintained in state-owned enterprises. After so many centuries of an apprenticeship system, Germans can't conceive of doing without apprentices. Every year, millions of young Germans enter the maw of corporate training programs, bound for the best-known corporations such as Siemens or Thyssen as well as for the local auto garage or bakery.

"Mother's Milk"

It's impossible to generalize about the type of student who enters an apprenticeship program, because the system accommodates just about everyone. The participants come from every part of the country and every socioeconomic background. Few challenge the apprenticeship system, and the majority find their work through it. Even the rebellious types can find a place in the system: rather than working for Deutsche Bank, they can become apprentice bakers or painters.

Today more than 500,000 companies offer apprenticeships in some 450 "officially recognized" professions. No company is required to provide such training, but all the large ones—including subsidiaries of foreign companies like Ford—and most of the smaller companies do. The companies typically provide separate facilities for apprentices. These may include workshops, classrooms, even a gym and recreational fields. If the company is small and of limited means, it can pool resources with other similar companies to provide common facilities.

The key to the apprenticeship philosophy is that every job, however menial it may seem, is considered part of a larger picture. Apprentices learn to think about what they are doing and how it fits into a larger scheme. In the schools they get some of the usual dose of culture like social studies or German, but they also learn the theoretical aspects of their chosen profession. An apprentice salesclerk learns about currency exchange rates and principles of taxation. A potential car mechanic is taught the engineering concepts of a car as well as the environmental risks posed by various car fluids and components. Germans want and expect a work force with no weak links, and apprenticeships are crucial in achieving that goal.

One criticism of the German apprenticeship system is that it is too rigid. A gifted car mechanic with a fine ear for engines must still pass various written exams before he can land a job. On the other hand, the image of the self-taught, self-made worker tends to be overglamorized. The United States prides itself on being the land of opportunity, and many "success stories" have indeed bootstrapped their way up from the mailroom. But think of the countless uneducated, unskilled—and unproductive—mailroom workers who stayed right there. Germany may not be known as the land of opportunity from the individual's standpoint, but the better-skilled work force as a whole benefits everyone.

Some of the most famous German managers, and even some heads of corporations, got their start as apprentices. The head of the Bayer chemicals company, Hermann Strenger, started out as an apprentice salesman. Uwe Thomsen, who is on the management board of Hoechst, was also once an apprentice salesman, and now he wholeheartedly endorses the system for his company: "What makes the character or corporate culture of a company is the people and the structure. If people know your system from the bottom up, they know your thinking process. It is a bit like mother's milk."

To the German employer, the apprentice's experience is essential; to the employee, it's unforgettable. Many find it frustrating and terrifying. All admit, though, that these programs offer the best training for business. Joachim Luerman is a consultant in New York today, but years ago he had this German apprenticeship experience: "They gave me a piece of metal, a file and a ruler and told me to spend the day making a five-centimeter cube. So I began filing away, thinking it was an easy task and that I'd soon be done. And then after a while I realized it was damn near impossible. My work piece got smaller and smaller, but never became a true cube. This taught me that without experience, even simple production jobs can cause difficulties."

Peter Weuling started his career at an old Hamburg-based trading company. "I remember the first or second day on the job they put me in a room to answer telexes. I was terrified because here were these telexes coming in from around the world—India, South America—written in English, and I had to acknowledge them. I wasn't sure about my English then, or how to use the machine properly, and I was terrified I would lose a client of the company. This experience was repeated in other areas, but in spite of all the horrors, I survived. Even though I'm no longer with the company, I still run across the people I knew as apprentices from time to time, and there's an instant rapport."

Because the apprenticeship offers not only professional skills but a business network to its participants, the competition to get into the best programs is quite high. Just as applicants take pains to choose the best employers, managers are looking for the best crop of apprentices they can find. With thousands of companies to choose from, and with some company programs considered better than others, competition can be as severe as it is for American high school students trying to get into Ivy League colleges. As one of Germany's leading corporations, the Hoechst chemicals company is certainly among the chosen companies. Based a few miles outside of downtown Frankfurt, Hoechst can afford to be selective in its admissions process. The procedure is not unlike applying to college. Hoechst publishes an information packet with a separate flyer explaining the parameters of each job—there are eighty in all—and the skills a prospective apprentice should have. The company sells itself: on one of the glossy sheets a smiling Christine Klement explains how she started as an apprentice in 1984 and what she has done at Hoechst since then. It's a bit hokey—almost every job description calls for "good teamwork skills"—but the process is certainly more rational than clipping want ads in the local paper.

The director of Hoechst's apprenticeships, Helmut Hofmann, says he offers apprenticeships to the best and the smartest regardless of their appearance or sociability. "When I interview prospective apprentices, I am more concerned with their ability to be punctual and get their assignments completed on time than with how they look. Maybe they are big on sports or computer freaks, that's okay." The emphasis Germans place on punctuality is one stereotype that is undeniably true. If a youth isn't punctual by age fifteen, the future is bleak.

Apprenticeship programs are structured in much the same way as a college curriculum. But the emphasis isn't on learning alone, it's also on application. Hoechst's apprenticeship center, a large building with the ubiquitous word *Ausbildung* ("training") plastered on the side, stands apart from the manufacturing facilities but is connected to them through numerous above-ground pipelines carrying basic chemicals and gases. The atmosphere is academic but less chaotic than your average campus. Supervised by a company *Meister* who offers occasional pointers, young male and female apprentices experiment with chemicals in a lab and record their observations. Across the hall, in the metal shop, the scene is similar. In another room, a roomful of young women pounds away on manual typewriters (word processors come later). The teacher, Frau Wolf, explains the all-female presence: "Unfortunately, the efforts that have been made to attract women to traditionally male professions have not worked in reverse."

The apprenticeship center uses other methods, both direct and indirect, to instill company values. Apprentices wear long gray lab coats emblazoned with the company name. In the metal shop hangs a mirror with the following message written across the top: "I too should feel responsible for safety on the job and protection of the environment." Just opposite the mirror stand separate bins for sorting different types of waste materials. A chart lists which can be recycled and which are hazardous and must be disposed of carefully.

First-year apprentices spend most of their time in the training center, but in the second and third years they may take on tasks on the shop floor. The foreman or shop steward then sees how the apprentice handles various tasks, and knows whether he wants to hire the apprentice eventually. About 95 percent of all apprentices completing the program are offered jobs with the company. The company pays a high price for the chance to train and choose its own people.

Hoechst employs a total of over 6,000 apprentices at thirty-two manufacturing plants in Germany. That comes to almost 7.5 percent of Hoechst's total work force in the country. The total cost amounts to nearly 15 percent of the company's annual net income—slightly under DM 25,000 per apprentice. Again, that works out to about the same as a year at Harvard.

Of course, not all of that money is paid to the apprentice. The average salary is only about DM 13,000 per year, not enough to live on. Most apprentices live at home anyway, though, and the extra money can be saved, used to buy a stereo or spent on traveling. The remaining DM 12,000 from the company goes to overhead costs of in-house schooling: teachers, equipment, the gym and recreational facilities.

Obviously not every employer can afford such lavish facilities as Hoechst can. It may be that a small country restaurant offers one or two apprenticeships for cooks, who spend their time working in the kitchen. The restaurant owner would still have to adhere to certain minimum standards, enforced by local chambers of commerce, to ensure that the apprentices don't spend their entire apprenticeship peeling potatoes. So the kids learn a wide range of skills involved in running a restaurant: cooking, purchasing, bookkeeping.

A Well-Rounded Country

For Germany as a whole, the benefits of this system are immense. Youth unemployment in Germany is lower than in most other industrial countries. Skilled, trained laborers are never in short supply. The high quality of German products is known worldwide. And this training, this respect, costs the German government almost nothing; the bills are footed by private enterprise.

The total cost of apprenticeship programs to German industry is estimated to be in the range of DM 20 billion (or approximately $12 billion) or one fourth the total amount of government spending on education, which in Germany includes primary schools as well as universities.

German corporations perform a delicate balancing act when it comes to programming their apprenticeships. On the one hand, they would prefer to train only those workers they will need. On the other, they recognize a certain social responsibility. In the late 1970s and early 1980s, when the nation was awash in maturing baby boomers, private enterprise paid a high price to keep the country's work force skilled. As Hans Ebmayer of the government Ministry of Education and Science points out: "We had 500,000 available apprenticeship spots and between 750,000 and 780,000 people needing a spot. The German economy managed to create 720,000 spots, an extraordinary achievement." Uwe Thomsen of Hoechst confirms the point: "About ten years ago we had the debate in this country that Hoechst and other companies exploited workers, but that discussion was ideological and almost demagogic. When the level of youth unemployment began to rise, German industry went to remarkable lengths to at least provide young people with basic vocational training and save them from an uncertain future."

Of course, German industry didn't go to extraordinary lengths to provide apprenticeships entirely out of altruism. Certain currents in the federal government, particularly in the Social Democratic party, as well as some unions have favored more direct governmental involvement in providing apprenticeships. This involvement would be financed by a tax on companies. But as Thomsen of Hoechst notes, "That danger no longer exists today," and German companies remain committed to providing apprenticeships for all comers.

The German government also did its part to accommodate the massive influx of apprentices by loosening the government's regulation of apprenticeship standards. At that point employers who had never been able to hire apprentices were suddenly flooded with applications. One restaurateur in southern Germany told how for years he had wanted to take on an apprentice or two but could not because in spite of his thirty-plus years' experience, he had not passed his *Meisterprüfung* ("master's exam"). The local chamber of commerce, which acts on behalf of the federal government to approve the hiring of apprentices, finally relented.

Today, the problem is reversed. There aren't enough apprentice-aged youths to go around. And of those who are there, fewer are interested in the more traditional professions like toolmaking. "Now all the kids want computer, computer, computer," says Ebmayer. The large companies like Hoechst will always find enough apprentices. The problem will lie mainly with the many medium-sized tool companies, which depend on skilled labor and are essential to Germany's export economy. The government Ministry of Education and Science has stepped up efforts to publicize the opportunities in such professions and make them more attractive to women, who have traditionally shied away from them.

The government is also involved in the accreditation and deaccreditation of "officially recognized professions." Given the system's long history, it has supported thousands of professions, many of which can easily outdate or outmodernize themselves, such as blacksmithing or milling. Just what constitutes a profession can be a matter of lengthy negotiation among business, government and unions. Some professions are very specialized. In the chemical field, for example, a chemical laboratory technician is not the same as a chemical industry production assistant. Technological change can eliminate some professions and create others. The metal industry recently concluded eight years of negotiations to simplify sixteen separate professions into five. Constant adaptation of a profession to the current job market is obviously crucial.

Spreading the Wealth

There are few downsides to the apprenticeship system. But in terms of labor costs, the system is no doubt a double-edged sword. While these intense training programs make Germany's labor force perhaps the most skilled in the world, they also create some of the highest labor expenses in the world. In the competitive global marketplace, many a foreign company—including many U.S. corporations—has moved its plants and factories to less expensive countries where labor is cheaper. German businesses also have this opportunity but are more reluctant to shift their manufacturing away from their skilled work force at home. They feel the homemade product is better. In this way, they are reliant on their own apprentice system. In cases where companies do move abroad to stay competitive, they try to bring along their training programs where feasible and welcome the local work force for schooling.

In Mexico, for example, the three major German chemical firms have essentially subsidized a joint school for teaching students according to German methods. The cost of facilities and teachers in Mexico is relatively cheap, so these companies can afford to pay for what would normally be a government expense. The German corporations put up money for the school, knowing very well that nothing prevents a young Mexican apprentice from getting the free education and going to work for someone else. Asked about that possibility, Uwe Thomsen of Hoechst replies: "It's not bad if they bring good memories of our companies with them. We have to contribute to the development of these countries, even if it costs us. Anyway, most stay with us." He speaks those closing words, "most stay with us," with an air of confidence that is typical of Germans. To an envious foreign competitor, it might be confused with arrogance.

This type of long-range planning comes naturally to the Germans, and it makes a good selling point in many foreign markets. The Eastern Europeans are well aware of the German system for learning and doing business. Thomsen travels throughout Eastern Europe for Hoechst, and as he puts it, "the word 'apprenticeship' is on everyone's lips." An Eastern European company might well choose a German partner that has the experience and facilities to train workers. There's no doubt that the few burgeoning private enterprises in East Berlin, Dresden and Leipzig, as well as Prague and Warsaw, could use some skilled workers and long-range thinkers. The German companies can fill that need.

Today's top German corporations can't always take their apprenticeship programs to the United States, where the cost of maintaining facilities and paying teachers is generally too high. Still, they would like to. When asked to compare the quality of German employees with those of a U.S. subsidiary, a German industrialist will typically skirt the issue in order to avoid causing trouble with the foreign staff. One midsize entrepreneur who recently established his company's first U.S. subsidiary was shocked by the lack of skills in the work force.

In New York City, the largest German banks and two Swiss banks have come together to take matters into their own hands. Their American trainees receive twenty months of practical training in the respective banks and take four months of general courses together at the American Institute of Banking. The curriculum focuses on the American banking system and on international banking, and is supervised by the German American Chamber of Commerce, which also issues a certificate comparable to what a German apprentice would get. The program is so successful that already other non-German banks are considering joining. Many U.S. subsidiaries of German companies would love to emulate the German banks, but since they are spread around the four corners of the country, the logistics are prohibitive.

In early 1991 Hans Decker, head of external relations for Siemens in the United States, wrote an op-ed piece for *The Wall Street Journal* in which he recommended that U.S. companies emulate the German apprenticeship system. But Decker later acknowledged that even Siemens had so far done little in the United States. To get the ball rolling, Decker maintains, companies from the same industrial sectors must first agree on a common curriculum, and "that takes time." Furthermore, says Decker, "You have to tell people that there's another option besides going to college and dropping out. That requires a certain selling job by the public authorities." Adopting the entire German dual system of education would be much too difficult in the United States, thinks Decker, but he notes that Siemens is looking to establish some programs in the United States using existing facilities such as community colleges and the like.

Some American companies have begun training a few apprentices, and the idea is also popular among politicians. But if one lesson can be learned from Germany, it is that corporate America should take the initiative ahead of the politicians. Only then will apprenticeship programs be more of an asset than a cost.

8

The Checks and Balances of German Corporate Power

The fall from grace of communism in the late 1980s in Eastern Europe and elsewhere in the world was also widely hailed as the triumph of "democratic capitalism," that winning combination of democracy in government and free enterprise in business. Just as Winston Churchill knew that democracy is the worst but only form of government, many erstwhile communists finally realized that capitalism is the worst but only form of economy for business. The only real problem with "democratic capitalism" is the term itself. It suggests that "democratic" modifies "capitalism," when in fact a capitalist business is usually far from democratic. When the boss says jump, employees jump, they don't take a vote. Ownership has its privileges.

The chain of command in a typical American capitalist corporation is, by and large, equally straightforward. The owner calls the shots, runs the business and hires the employees, or else hires managers to run the business and hire the employees. In the large public corporation without a single identifiable owner, the shareholders elect a board of managers to represent their interests. A simple diagram of such an arrangement would show the board of directors on top, the executives and managers in the middle and the employees on the bottom. Power begins at the top and flows downward.

German corporations are different. Power ultimately flows downward from the owners, of course, but numerous checks and balances set up along the way make the chain of command much more tangled; owners, as a result, do not necessarily control the firm. The winners in this zero-sum power game usually turn out to be the managers—and to a lesser extent the employees.

Complaints about entrenched management are by no means unique to Germany. Even in the United States, the land of unfettered capitalism, shareholders frequently gripe about their lack of influence on the managers of their company. A cry went up at shareholders' organizations not long ago when Sears, Roebuck's management reduced the number of seats on its board from fifteen to ten. The move looked an awful lot like a simple power play designed to keep a disgruntled shareholder from gaining a seat.

German managements are dug in even deeper than their U.S. counterparts, however, and German shareholders have a much harder time making themselves heard. In large part, that's because Germans believe that an entrenched management is the price you pay for corporate stability. Let the shareholders have their way, the thinking goes, and pretty soon German companies will fall into the trap that plagues the American corporation: quarterly rather than semiannual earnings reports, a volatile stock price, a focus on short-term results, the whole show.

While this line of thinking has allowed German companies to pursue carefully-thought-out long-term plans with notable success, it can be used by management to mask underperformance; German managers are frequently accountable to no one but themselves. The situation is aggravated by Germany's "dual-board" system, a system markedly different from the simple board of directors common in the United States and Britain.

Managing by Committee

The board of directors of an American corporation presumably represents the shareholders' interests and stands alone at the top. The board's makeup can vary considerably from company to company, as does the distribution of power. When the firm's chief executive and board chairman are one and the same—as Tom Watson was at IBM or Lee Iacocca at Chrysler—he can really put his personal stamp on the company. Other instances abound, however, where the chief executive finds himself at the mercy of an independent-minded board. In 1991, when the Compaq computer company began showing a downturn in sales and earnings after eight straight years of record growth, the board axed Rod Canion, its longtime chief executive, before the year was out. In 1992, the board of General Motors asserted itself in dramatic fashion by curtailing the powers of chief executive Robert Stempel.

German corporations boast two boards: a supervisory board, which represents shareholders and oversees management, and a management board. Essentially a German creation, the latter consists of the chief executive and other leading company executives —usually the chief financial officer, the controller, the heads of personnel, sales and other functions—who act together as a unit. The idea behind a separate management board lies in an emphasis on the distinction between the company's management and its supervision. By law, members of a firm's management board may not sit on its supervisory board.

At first glance, the German dual-board system may appear to give the upper hand to the supervisory board in any ultimate struggle to guide the course of the firm. After all, the emphasis on collegiality among the members of the management board means that, unlike many American CEOs, few German CEOs have the power to dominate a firm. Even in those cases in which the German CEO is "more equal" than his colleagues on the management board, he still cannot represent his views on the supervisory board. But the reality, more often than not, is just the opposite: the German management board is very powerful indeed.

Several factors come into play in weakening the power of the German supervisory boards. For starters, they meet only four times a year (compare that to the average eight annual meetings of U.S. boards of directors). And their power is easily eviscerated by the system of crossholdings so dear to the hearts of German businessmen. Because so many German banks and industrial companies hold stakes of 5 percent or more in other companies—collectively forming a sort of huge daisy chain—the supervisory boards tend to be filled from a limited pool of candidates. Many supervisory board members rotate from company to company, sitting on as many as twenty or more boards at a time, a syndrome most common among German bankers. Since banks and industrial concerns generally make most of their profits from their own operations—and not from dividends received from their stakes in other firms—executives focus far more on their own companies than they do on the companies on whose supervisory boards they happen to sit.

Collegiality in the management board has many beneficial effects. Above all, decisions reached by consensus can often be implemented with more vigor than those rammed through by some egomaniacal chief executive. But in practice, collegiality can have the entrenching effect of a steam shovel: lines of authority and responsibility frequently become muddled. When business turns bad, it becomes harder to single out the culprit without indicting the group. And since managers typically sign multiyear employment contracts, it can be quite expensive to buy them out.

Peter Harf, of the consumer products firm Benckiser, is an astute observer of German business. His angle on the power of the management boards is acute: "As long as the company makes enough money to survive, it becomes virtually impossible to displace any member of the board. Legally speaking, there are five or six equal partners. What options do they have? Do they single out one person who is not achieving the best possible results and tell the supervisory board, 'Okay, kill this guy'? Do so, and they weaken their own position. Attack one, and you establish a precedent. So the management boards band together, not necessarily to run the company better, but to defend themselves against shareholders. They tend to build independent empires. They work hard to keep the whole system immune from outsiders, and they make things bureaucratic. Then the system is perpetuated because the management boards recruit new members from within the firm.''

Managing by Consensus

If all these factors were not enough, the problem of weak supervisory boards is exacerbated by the infamous laws of codetermination, which mandate employee representation on supervisory boards in numbers equal to representatives of capital interests. Through these laws Germany appears to have gone further than any other capitalist country in empowering the ordinary worker. The world turned upside down? Ordinary employees supervising the work of their bosses on the management boards? What sounds like a revolutionary idea in fact turns out to be a snore.

Employee representatives on supervisory boards tend to be quite docile. Even if they felt inclined to make things difficult for the capital interests, the tie-breaking system works to the advantage of those capital interests. What at first blush seems to constitute a bold move to empower the workers fizzles in practice. Moreover, the presence of employee representatives on the supervisory boards actually further solidifies the entrenchment of management. In his book *Success Through Partnership*, Reinhard Mohn, the fifth-generation entrepreneur to run the family-owned media company Bertelsmann AG, describes the problem with codetermination:

> Polarization of capital and labor dominates the field. Neither side wants to risk losing in the voting process because of internal dissent. Accordingly, the most important decisions are already prepared in separate meetings of capital and labor. Dissenting opinions of individual members of the supervisory board are no longer appropriate at the meeting of the entire supervisory board—unless that member wants to jeopardize his mandate.

As a logical consequence, the managing boards are less and less interested in dialogue with the supervisory board, a dialogue which could be very helpful to them. They doubt the competence of many supervisory board members and attempt, usually success-fully, to escape its supervision.

Mohn is hardly the archcapitalist, antiworker type; he is a successful businessman looking to reinstill the entrepreneurial spirit into the German corporation. The only way to do that, says Mohn, is to shake up managers and make them think more like owners—a highly unlikely scenario under the current board sys-tem.

While there is occasional grumbling about codetermination in German business circles, no widespread revolt has taken place. One reason: codetermination represents a hard-fought victory for the German labor movement, which has consistently been eager to prove itself a responsible partner in Germany's economic suc-cess.

The history of codetermination goes back decades. In the Ger-man coal and steel industry, labor representatives have shared equal voting rights on company supervisory boards with outside directors ever since the end of the Second World War. For all other large German companies of over two thousand employees, labor has been represented on the boards in near equality since 1976. The idea of putting labor on supervisory boards in Germany predated the war, but implementation came only under the influ-ence of the Allied occupying powers, who wanted to ensure that the German coal and steel industrialists, who had all too eagerly provided the Nazis with the raw materials for armaments, would be kept in check. To be extra sure, they sentenced the guiltiest of the industrialists, Friedrich Flick, Alfried Krupp and Hermann Röchling, to prison sentences, while a fourth, Albert Vögler, swallowed poison. The remaining coal and steel industrialists agreed to labor participation in the supervisory boards if only to prevent nationalization of their firms.

The impact of codetermination in the early years was not as revolutionary as some might have expected, largely because labor lacked the experience—and perhaps the desire—to push for radical changes. The labor contingent on the various company supervisory boards seldom, if ever, tried to block certain managers from being promoted to the management board. Similarly, management was able to pursue mergers and acquisitions without interference from the labor supervisors. Most telling, labor did not fundamentally obstruct the necessary elimination of hundreds of thousands of jobs in coal and steel during the 1960s and 1970s.

On the management side, there was little joy in the coal and steel companies at being supervised by labor. In addition to seats on a company's supervisory board, labor was given a say in the choice of the personnel representative on the management board, the *Arbeitsdirektor*. This labor infiltration led to some amusing turf wars. In his book *Erste Garnitur,* Hans Otto Eglau tells how Hans-Günther Sohl, the longtime chief executive of Thyssen, took the responsibility for publishing the company bulletin away from the *Arbeitsdirektor* on the grounds that it might be read by the clients (and therefore should reflect the viewpoint of management, not labor). Ultimately, however, as one unnamed but highly placed banker pointed out, "Sohl did not run his company any differently than he would have without codetermination."

Having at any rate succeeded in not rocking the boat, labor representatives could claim that they were responsible folks who were qualified to continue sitting on the supervisory boards. The idea of extending codetermination to all large German corporations generated heated debates in the German parliament in the 1970s, but was finally passed in 1976, during the tenure of Social Democrat Helmut Schmidt as chancellor. Even so, the law allowed for major differences with the coal and steel industry: supervisory boards are not subject to full parity, and the chairman of the board, who represents shareholders, has two votes and can break any deadlock (in the coal and steel industry, deadlocks are broken by a neutral board member acceptable to both sides). Moreover, the 1976 law did not give labor a say in the choice of an *Arbeitsdirektor*.

For all of German labor's success at getting a hand on the corporate tiller through codetermination, the effort may be due for a reversal of sorts. As the EC moves to eliminate hidden trade barriers and create a truly common market, companies will presumably be able to do business in the lucrative German market without setting up there. Codetermination will certainly make foreign companies think twice before setting up in Germany, especially since no other European country seems prepared to emulate the German system.

In the same vein, if a company can in fact be governed from anywhere in the EC, what is to prevent the exodus of German companies who find codetermination not to their liking? Some signs of such a trend have already appeared. Jörg Barczynski of the IG Metall union points out that General Motors, whose European operations had been governed since 1925 through the wholly owned subsidiary Adam Opel AG in Rüsselsheim, about fifteen miles southwest of Frankfurt, switched its headquarters to Switzerland in 1982. Now Opel still has codetermination in Rüsselsheim, but the parent GM in Switzerland does not. A spokesman for Opel would say only that GM wanted to move its headquarters to a neutral site—a country where GM did not manufacture at all—and that Switzerland was centrally located.

When the Hannover-based Pelikan office supply and furniture company faced possible bankruptcy in 1983, the company was bailed out by the Metro group. With sales over DM 40 billion, Metro is today one of Europe's leading chain of wholesale stores; its nominal headquarters are in Switzerland. Company founder Otto Beisheim was originally German, but he moved himself and Metro to Switzerland. Six years and three chief executives after the bailout, Pelikan was restructured into seven separate legal entities, even though the furniture operations remained under the same roof in Hannover. One effect of the restructuring: no one division had more than 2,000 workers, and, presumably, the 1976 codetermination law no longer applied. Out went the separate Pelikan supervisory board—and codetermination along with it.

Cases like Opel and Pelikan are still the exceptions, although many German entrepreneurs, if not about to pack up and move abroad, are clearly dissatisfied with the direction of codetermination. These entrepreneurs feel the unions have already secured a high standard of living for the German workers, and that now they simply want power. Werner Otto, it may be recalled, praised the unions for raising the standard of living for workers, but he also added a caveat: too much union involvement in decision making can be counterproductive, even dangerous.

No one outside Germany is particularly interested in adopting German-style codetermination. Most U.S. managers and shareholders would take up Buddhism before they agreed to put labor representatives on their boards. Chrysler did in fact give one board seat (out of eighteen) to the head of the United Auto Workers in 1980, an arrangement planned as a payback for the UAW's agreement to wage cuts when Chrysler was on the ropes. But in early 1991, Chrysler claimed it was "cutting costs" by trimming five seats from the board, including the UAW's. In the United States, even when employees own company stock through increasingly popular employee stock ownership plans (ESOPs), their board representation is kept to a minimum. In Europe, while labor has a voice on the boards of some companies, Germany remains far ahead of its neighbors in this respect.

Even if the principle of codetermination does not catch on in other countries, the Germans will no doubt stick with it. On some level, codetermination serves as a pacifier for labor: seats on the supervisory board give labor the illusion of participating in the larger questions affecting the company and reinforce the notion of equality among the people at the top of a company and those at the bottom. Ask Jörg Barczynski of IG Metall what qualifies an ordinary worker to sit on a supervisory board, and he replies with another question: "What qualifies a manager to tell a worker how to use a wrench?"

The labor representatives are no dummies. They too know that real power is held by the management boards. The unions have lobbied to attain more influence there, but without success. It's an issue on which the battle lines have been drawn clearly; if German management finds itself in a very strong position vis-à-vis capital interests, it is by no means as powerful in the face of labor, and is not prepared to make any concessions.

Managing by Council

Every German firm with more than five employees is required to organize and maintain an employee council. The councils, consisting of elected representatives from the labor force, help oversee internal company policies and keep open the lines of communication with management. In the best cases the employee council is respected by management and contributes to improvements in production methods and productivity. In the worst cases the employee councils cannot even get management to serve chicken salad in the canteen on Thursdays. But even in such cases, employee councils are a force that management cannot completely ignore.

The concept of an employee council is not unique to German firms. Companies in France, Italy and several other European countries have similar arrangements. In the United States, the United Auto Workers union has approved a few contracts with auto manufacturers requiring full-time shop stewards—people responsible for labor relations on the factory floor—but the concept of an employee council remains by and large alien to U.S. firms. The German system is all-embracing: any company with more than five employees is officially expected to designate an employee as the employee council. At that level, of course, no one really cares. One Frankfurt securities broker laughed when reminded of the law: "Gee, that's right. We have twenty people in our firm and no designated employee." The rules get more serious for companies with over 300 employees: such firms must have at least one employee working full time just on council matters. The more employees, the greater the number of employee council members, and the largest German companies may have 40 or 50 people working full time on council business alone.

What do all these people do? Some tasks are as banal as suggesting improvements in the company canteen. Others are more complex. Council representatives are elected by their worker peers for terms of three years, during which time they talk regularly with management. For example, management may ask for more overtime in a certain department. The employee council responds, this is the fourth time in four months we've been asked to work more overtime; can't we hire more workers? Management says no, we don't have enough machines to support a bigger work force. Well, the council responds, can't we get new machines? And so it goes. Such dialogues are not merely pro forma, since the council has very real powers. Under German corporate law, management cannot hire, fire or require overtime work without the approval of the employee council. American managers reading this will no doubt scream "Egad!" (or something less printable), and not a few German managers curse and spit as it is.

In reality, however, the power of the employee councils is more of a hurdle than an obstacle. If management wants to fire someone and the council disapproves, the matter is referred to a federal labor court. There, management need only show that the employee is coming in late, abusing his sick days or whatever, and the case will be rapidly decided in management's favor. Similarly, the council cannot block management from investing in a machine that takes away jobs or prevent management from laying off workers in difficult times. The councils are by no means Trojan horses for the unions.

That said, the unions do present a list of recommended candidates at election time, and both the unions and the employee councils are concerned with many of the same social issues. In a typical well-managed company, however, the councils pledge allegiance to the firm first, not the unions. If management fires a worker for being continually late, neither the council nor the union will stand in the way. But if the council believes a particular union demand will harm a company's competitiveness, the council members will not simply back the union blindly. On the contrary, employee councils have been known to chew out the unions for making unrealistic demands. Finally, with elections held every three years, the council members are held accountable.

The sharing of power on this level of the German corporation is designed to force management to work with its employees, not against them. At lot of time is spent—some would say wasted— on internal company negotiations. These negotiations can be a great advantage, however: lots of discussion and debate take place within the company before any decision is implemented, so subsequent dissent is greatly reduced. Furthermore, once a year, management has to present to the employee council a kind of "state of the company" report bearing on financial results, productivity, investment plans and the like. The information divulged is far more detailed than the meager handouts to the financial community or the press. As a result, the system can work smoothly only if each side trusts the other absolutely.

While the system of employee councils has by and large functioned well in Germany, possible changes are already on the horizon. Several German auto manufacturers—among them Volkswagen and Opel—have begun emulating the Japanese system of group work along the assembly line. Workers are split up into groups, given a series of tasks to accomplish and left to their own devices to portion out the work. The idea is that greater productivity results when an assembly line worker is not stuck mounting headlights every day, but instead gets to mount headlights one day and install batteries the next. Another presumed advantage of group work: once management sets the overall production goal, peer pressure within the group ensures that the targets are met. So absenteeism decreases and productivity goes up. If the system proves successful in Germany—and it's still too early to tell—such groups may de facto replace the employee councils in importance.

A greater threat to the employee council may come from the increasing decentralization of business across European national borders. Because most German firms have traditionally kept their feet planted firmly on German soil, with perhaps a few distribution and sales subsidiaries abroad, the employee council could always stay close to the action. But German firms are increasingly setting up manufacturing facilities abroad—and more and more foreign firms are buying into German manufacturing. Either way, the relative importance of the employee councils will diminish—unless, of course, the system can be re-created elsewhere.

At European Community headquarters in Brussels, union representatives from various countries have been lobbying head to head with their management counterparts over a proposed EC-wide system of employee councils. One EC proposal calls for a central employee council to be based at company headquarters whenever a company has over 100 employees and significant operations in at least two EC countries. Further, at least one council member would have to come from each country where the company does business. Not surprisingly, management lobbyists are horrified. They fear a bureaucratic nightmare that would add little to the management of the company. From the German perspective, the thought of dealing with employee council members who have ties to the more militant unions in other European countries is even less encouraging. Where German corporate law on employee councils speaks of "cooperation based on trust," the European version is ominously silent.

With all the tips of the hat to labor, the lines of corporate power in Germany remain clearly drawn. They allow for a degree of social involvement unknown in most other developed economies. And it is unlikely that further integration with Germany's European neighbors will water down either the power or the involvement.

9

Comfort and Terror in the Life
of the German Executive

So far, we have looked at German companies—and the German business climate in general—as a reasonably well coordinated "social market" economy with its ethical roots in a large group of small and medium-size companies that maintain close ties with their communities, their unions and their bankers. But what of the German business executives, the men (women are few) who run those businesses, large and small? In the United States, those men (and women) are the stars of the show: receiving top billing in the business press and in the eyes of the general public in terms of fame as well as money, some have even attained a kind of celebrity status. If Lee Iacocca and Michael Milken haven't quite reached Madonna's exalted heights, they're not all that far off.

Germany is different. Naturally, the movements of the Carl Hahns and others who run Germany's top corporations are closely followed in the press—and their popularity as a target of terrorism doesn't help—but the average top executive in Germany actively shuns such attention. Who are the men (and the occasional women) running Germany's businesses, and how do they live?

Another Day, Another Deutsche Mark

Nowhere is the contrast between the German business executive and his American counterpart more starkly highlighted than in the matter of compensation. In the United States the compensation of a public corporation's executive officers is spelled out for all to see right there in the annual proxy statement. The major business magazines then splash across their pages four-color glossy pictures of the best-paid chief executives, with their salary totals, bonuses and profits from stock options and the like calculated down to the nearest penny. So everyone knows that in 1990 Steve Ross of Time Warner earned some $3.2 million in salary and bonus and another $57 million from the sale of stock. The year before, the winner was Craig McCaw of McCaw Cellular; by exercising 1.5 million stock options, he pulled in almost $54 million, even though his salary and bonus that year were a paltry $289,000, well below the average for the top chief executives. Giving stock and stock options to the CEO and other top executives, frequently couched in terms of "pay for performance," is still a popular form of compensation in American corporations, and ultimately the most rewarding. Straight salaries and bonuses, though, can also be quite high: Paul Fireman, the CEO of sneaker manufacturer Reebok, earned over $14 million a year for several years without including any extras at all.

Whether the superstar salaries of American CEOs are spiraling out of control depends on one's perspective. Most CEOs see the spectacular numbers racked up by their counterparts at other corporations and ask, "Why not me?" Not a few business observers, meanwhile, have come to see the issue of "pay for performance" as a thinly disguised veil for corporate greed. An article in the April 18, 1990, edition of *The Wall Street Journal,* a newspaper normally known for its pro-anything-free-market stance, had this to say: "The free-market value of top managers has been grossly inflated by prattle about the rarity of their talents."

Forbes magazine, also pro-free-market to the core, reflected a more belated change in attitude. In May 1990, *Forbes* was still spinning the party line: "Sure there are abuses in chief executive pay scales . . . but those who create wealth are entitled to share in it. That's what a market economy is all about." Exactly one year later, the magazine did a complete about-face. "One thing is clear: The current system, under which some people are paid in the tens of millions of dollars, even in the face of mediocre results, encourages little except cynicism."

By comparison, Germany has no such star system for its CEOs. One reason is that executive power, typically invested in the collegial management board, is more diffuse. The official title of the CEO of Deutsche Bank, for example, is "Speaker" of the management board. Nor does German corporate law require the disclosure of individual compensation, only the lump sum of the management board's compensation as a whole. Thus an outsider is privy only to the average compensation of all the managing board members. Although the exact figures for the highest-paid executives are hard to come by, they are clearly more modest than in the United States. One reason is that currently corporate stock is seldom given to German executives, as such remuneration is inefficient under the tax code.

In 1990 the German magazine *!Forbes von Burda* did estimate that the highest-paid executive was Peter Tamm of the Axel Springer corporation with DM 5 million, or around $3 million. Not bad, but then a German doctor is capable of making just as much. Furthermore, after Tamm with his DM 5 million and a handful of other top-paid executives, the numbers fall off dramatically, with most of the leading CEOs earning in the DM 1 million range. It's worth noting that many German executives have criticized the *!Forbes von Burda* estimates as far off the mark—presumably too high—but either way the Germans bring home far less than the Americans. The idea of pay for performance appeals to the Germans, though, and the trend is definitely heading toward greater incentives, through either bonuses or some kind of stock or participation certificates. Currently the typical German CEO's compensation is 80 percent fixed and 20 percent variable.

While German executives may want more pay-for-performance incentives, they are not necessarily looking to bring home as much as the Americans. Well, they may want to, but something deep inside them keeps murmuring that it's unhealthy. Peter Harf, who heads the privately owned Benckiser consumer products company (and who disputes the *!Forbes von Burda* estimate of his compensation as DM 1.6 million), says, "I'm very happy with my salary, and I don't want to make more. I mean, I'm greedy, and certainly if I have a chance to I will, but I don't think I should have a chance to." Harf also discounts the notion that a chief executive who turns a company around or dramatically improves a company's performance should be paid the lion's share of the profits: "What about the one hundred and fifty other guys who did their part too?"

Nor do typical German executives live the high life, flying around in jets to play golf or to visit their weekend homes; most of the leading corporations don't even have a jet (they charter one when necessary). The tax authorities monitor such perks closely to ensure they are for official business only. In short, German businessmen either avoid or simply don't have access to the privileges of so many of their counterparts in the United States, where the chief executive is both richly rewarded with money and given wide leeway for mixing personal and company business.

Indeed, German executives are so reserved that any exception to the rule stands out. Helmut Lohr was the chief executive of Stuttgart-based SEL AG from 1976 until 1989, when he was caught with his hand in the cookie jar one too many times. Lohr liked to live it up with company money, jetting to his vacation house on the Spanish island of Mallorca, redoing his house, driving about in fancy limousines and the rest. Eventually he was arrested for tax evasion and breach of trust (flights to his vacation home, for example, were listed in company expense accounts as domestic business trips).

Many of Lohr's activities probably would have gone unnoticed in the United States, where corporate chiefs seem to live like sultans. The same goes for Japan, where the modest salaries are offset by astronomical corporate expense accounts. Not in Germany, and especially not in Stuttgart. At Lohr's trial, his lawyers put forth the arguments that he was on duty for SEL around the clock, 365 days a year, and that many of the expenses were justifiable. No way, said the judge, since other SEL executives are on duty around the clock as well, and they cannot write off their personal expenses. The judge admonished Lohr, saying, "You are no better and no worse than the normal citizen." Indeed. Lohr was sentenced to three years in jail and fined.

That Germans do not have an executive star system is completely consistent with the German emphasis on building a company from the ground up: better to spend the money training apprentices than rewarding some executive with wealth far beyond what he needs to live comfortably. In this respect, German business is excellent proof that the power and honor of getting to the top are reward enough. Consider too that with the Red Army Faction—the terrorist group that specializes in the kidnapping and murder of business executives—still running amok, the higher a German executive climbs on the corporate ladder, the greater his chances of death by bullet. Even so, there is never a shortage of willing candidates. What's more, the honor and prestige of heading a major German corporation are nowhere near as great as in, say, Japan, where a top executive like Akio Morita of Sony can be practically deified. Yet the Japanese do not waste extravagant sums on their top executives, either.

All in a Day's Work

The lack of executives chasing big money in Germany also has a reverse effect: a lack of big money chasing executives willing to jump ship for the right price. The sheer number of German CEOs who got to the top spot by working their way up through the ranks of their respective corporations places a natural brake on the sort of executive shuffling so common in the United States. There are some notable exceptions, however, and switching companies in Germany does not have the treasonous implications that it might in Japan. Alfred Herrhausen worked for the electric utility VEW before being lured to Deutsche Bank. Carl Hahn worked for Volkswagen, then became CEO of the Continental AG tire company before returning to the top post at VW. The CEO of Porsche, Arno Bohn, was brought over from Nixdorf computer. In the chemicals industry, however, the top men have all come from within, and it is an unwritten rule that they will continue to do so. Siemens has also always found talent in house. Corporate loyalty in Germany, while not a binding straitjacket, still counts.

As German executives rise through the ranks of their respective corporations, they do so largely on the basis of their work at the company and not on old school ties or some other kind of old-boy network. Germany simply does not have the elite schools like the Ivy League in the United States, "Oxbridge" in England or Tokyo University in Japan. German universities are democratic and overcrowded; exclusive fraternities where drinking beer and dueling with untipped swords (not, one hopes, simultaneously) are age-old rites of passage are about as far as the university bonding experience goes. But while these fraternal bonds may carry over into professional life—one fellow may help a chum get a job or an interview—their actual significance is quite tame. Freemasons they are not.

In the business world, advanced degrees are not essential, although most executives have them. One of the most popular German degrees is a doctorate in engineering. The ranks of German executives are filled with holders of these degrees, which helps explain the German emphasis on technical excellence. Indeed, the preferred German solution to improving a company is to build a better product, an approach that has served German business well. Much has been written about the need for American companies to build higher-quality products, and recruiting more engineers for the executive suites is one oft-mentioned solution. At the same time, many German companies are looking for executives with stronger marketing and financial backgrounds, never German strengths. Thus more and more students are choosing business school or going abroad to pursue an M.B.A.

German business schools lag well behind the competition abroad. The local school with perhaps the best reputation is not in Germany at all, but in neighboring Switzerland: the *Hochschule St. Gallen*. In Germany the *Hochschule für Unternehmensführung* in

Koblenz has a good reputation, but neither of these schools has the clout of a Harvard or Stanford M.B.A. or a degree from the INSEAD in France. For Germans, who are used to free education, one problem with all of these schools is cost.

If a young German cannot afford a private school like Koblenz or get a scholarship to attend Harvard, he or she can still get a doctorate from any of the German state universities in *Betriebswirtschaftslehre*—a cross between business administration and economics. The German doctorate is actually easier to obtain than an American Ph.D., and the advantage is that the holder is thereafter entitled to be referred to as "Herr Doktor" (or "Frau Doktor"), which sounds pretty good to some people.

Still, whether the student receives a doctorate in business or engineering, or a business school degree, the end result is often the same. German companies assume they will have to teach new recruits everything they need to know anyway, through either an apprenticeship or some other form of training.

To say that German business is free of an old-boy network based on past school ties is not to say that there is no old-boy network at all. But the network is not cultivated until middle age, usually after a young executive has worked his way well up the corporate ladder. The multiple corporate crossholdings and reciprocal seats on company supervisory boards that characterize German business tend to create an elite circle of managers, perhaps between 150 and 200 throughout Germany. Not surprisingly, these power brokers are quite clubby with one another. And since Germany avoids "unfriendly" takeovers like the plague, executives must remain on very "friendly" terms with the people ahead of them in order to get to the top: the American syndrome of the cigar-chomping redneck who buys his way into fashionable circles with truckloads of borrowed cash is quite impossible in Germany—it's just not done.

Nor have many women succeeded in cracking the upper echelons of German business. A woman might make it onto a supervisory board if she has inherited a sizable chunk of the company's stock or by being appointed for her competence in other areas, but seldom for having worked her way up through the ranks of a major industrial corporation. Right now, the most visible woman in German business is Birgit Breuel, and she began as a politician.

In 1991, Breuel took over as head of the Treuhandanstalt, the agency responsible for privatizing former East German businesses, after Detlev Rohwedder was assassinated. Before that she earned her stripes as finance minister of the German state of Lower Saxony. Of course, she was not a complete stranger to the business world: her father, Alwin Münchmeyer, had been one of Germany's most influential and respected bankers.

Another route for women: building their own businesses. Jil Sander has done particularly well in this regard: she turned a small fashion design business into a public corporation that today sells fashion and cosmetics with over DM 100 million in sales.

Women, however, do populate the middle management ranks of German business in increasing numbers. But as in most other countries, German women hit the glass ceiling that limits upward mobility. Conditions may have evolved since the last century, when a woman's three prime responsibilities were *Kinder, Küche und Kirche* (children, kitchen and church). But what's a feminist to do about the prominent German chief executive who says that when considering a younger man for a promotion, he likes to meet both the man and his wife, "to see whether the wife stands by her man"?

German business is by and large a man's world. Even on quasi-social-business occasions—the client dinners, for example—Germans tend to leave the wives behind. Is that because of a desire to exclude women or because the German tax authorities monitor expense accounts so strictly?

Until recently, the German business elite has also been pretty much made up of Germans, with perhaps the odd Austrian or Swiss slipping through. This parochialism is not as pervasive as it is in Japan, where even a foreigner with a sizable stake in a company is often denied a vote on the board. German supervisory boards have long been open to foreigners. But at the management board level, where the real power lies, executives have tended to be almost exclusively German.

Lately, though, the ranks of some leading German management boards have opened up to foreigners. John Craven, South African by birth, went to Deutsche Bank after working at London's Morgan Grenfell brokerage house. Giuseppe Vita of Italy is now chief executive at Schering AG. Daniel Goeudevert, who is

French, went to Volkswagen after stints at Citroën and Ford in Germany. Pol Bamelis of Belgium now sits on the management board of Bayer. This trend is sure to continue as German firms increase their foreign direct investment through acquisitions abroad, instead of relying too heavily on exports.

Unquestionably, this crossbreeding in German executive circles can only help. The German obsession with privacy might relax a bit, and corporate disclosure will have to become more accessible to foreigners. By the same token, many of the strengths of German business, the socially minded thinking, the constructive relationship between management and labor, the apprenticeship system, the quality standards, will themselves be more readily apparent to people outside of Germany. The contrast with the Japanese, who seem far less willing to admit foreigners into their highest power circles, is noteworthy in this respect.

One would think that the emphasis German companies place on foreign assignments for their executives would create a more cosmopolitan perspective when these executives finally make it back home. Compared to American executives, who all too often have not lived abroad and who therefore tend to focus on their own vast internal market, the German executive would seem to be a paragon of internationalism. The truth, however, is somewhat more complex. As the German-born New York–based consultant Joachim Luerman points out: "Quite a few Germans come over to the U.S. and think that they are dealing with just another foreign country as they are used to in Europe. More often than not, they forget that they are dealing with a country that is the size of an entire continent." Sending a German abroad is no guarantee that he will come back smarter or more cosmopolitan, especially in a domestic business climate with its own strong traditions and prejudices.

To their credit, though, almost all German executives have gained at least a working knowledge of English, without question the international language of business. Many speak the language fluently, and corporate meetings in Germany that include foreigners are often held with English as the working language, even if Germans outnumber foreigners 99 to 1. That said, foreigners doing a lot of business with Germans should not be lulled into thinking that there is no point in learning at least a few words of

German. Most foreigners who have made the effort *ein bißchen Deutsch zu sprechen* report that it enables them to gain the trust of their German colleagues quickly. Like anyone else, Germans are flattered when a foreigner takes the time to learn their language. And Germans are quite tolerant of foreigners mangling the language of Goethe.

German executives may not be stars, but they are an excellent value for their companies. The model of the German executive—technically well educated, well paid without being spoiled—is certainly an attractive feature of German business. The American star system works well when the chief executive actually succeeds in achieving those stellar results, but all too often the executive gets megacompensation in spite of mediocre performance. Then management-labor relations are affected, since laying off employees or freezing salary levels sows seeds of resentment against the executive. In Germany, a little modesty in the executive suites goes a long way.

Unfortunately, there's a catch. For all his modesty, his reasonable salary and his concern for his employees, the German business executive has been the primary target of terrorist groups for well over a decade now. Organized terrorism, restricted in the United States to accounts in newspapers and TV, remains very much on the minds of German businessmen.

Terrorists at Work

Sitting in a Stuttgart courtroom in the spring of 1991, Susanne Albrecht was again Susanne Albrecht. Less than a year earlier, she had been Ingrid Jäger, an assistant in a chemical laboratory living a quiet life with her husband and daughter in East Berlin. For her, reunification did not mean potential unemployment; it meant a certain jail sentence. She was one of the most wanted criminals in West Germany, a member of the Red Army Faction terrorist organization. She was one of around ten ex-terrorists rounded up after the border between the two Germanies opened up, and her Stuttgart trial attracted the most attention: Susanne Albrecht's story was not just about terrorism; it was also about betrayal.

In July 1977, Susanne Albrecht, Brigitte Mohnhaupt and Christian Klar went to call on Jürgen Ponto. On the way, Albrecht took all the bullets out of her gun. The purpose of the visit was to abduct Ponto, then head of the Dresdner Bank, and use their hostage to force the release of several jailed RAF members, including Andreas Baader, a founder of the group. Susanne Albrecht was not exactly a hard-core member of the gang, but because she knew Ponto personally through her family—he was "Onkel Jürgen" to her—she was clearly the key to the operation.

Albrecht had been raised in an upstanding middle-class family in Hamburg. Her father was a successful maritime lawyer. In the early 1970s, the young woman, then in her twenties, became increasingly disenchanted with the system. She befriended squatters in Hamburg and happened to be in one of their buildings when the police came and forcefully cleared the house. This and other events instilled in her a case of middle-class guilt regarding the underprivileged. Increasingly estranged from her family, she began hanging out with members of the Red Army Faction. But she never completely lost touch with her mother.

Susanne Albrecht told the judge in the spring of 1991 that she had always felt like an outsider in the midst of the RAF, as if they never really trusted her. Perhaps that made her that much more eager to prove herself. When the members of the RAF learned that she personally knew Jürgen Ponto, they began pumping her for information. She claims she never wanted to harm the family friend, but the other RAF members insisted that they would simply abduct Ponto in the street if she refused to help. Such a kidnapping could get messy, they warned. Albrecht agreed to help.

Jürgen Ponto no doubt thought it strange when Albrecht called one day in the spring of 1977 to say she absolutely had to visit before he and his wife left for a vacation in South America. The Pontos had heard from Albrecht's mother that the troubled young woman had recently renewed contact with her family, but they could not know the real reason. On that fateful day, Ponto's chauffeur was surprised when two unannounced people showed up with Susanne at the gate. "How are they dressed?" asked Jürgen Ponto's wife. "Very stylishly," answered the chauffeur. Ponto's wife later recalled that Brigitte Mohnhaupt was dressed in yellow from head to toe, while Christian Klar looked like a store mannequin, elegantly coiffed head and all. The roses Susanne Albrecht brought had already begun to wilt. Once in the house,

Klar pulled a gun and told Ponto he was being kidnapped. The strong-willed Ponto told the kidnappers they were crazy and resisted. Klar and Mohnhaupt then both repeatedly shot Ponto, who fell to the dining room floor. The would-be kidnappers fled.

The botched kidnapping definitively changed Susanne Albrecht's life. Even if the other RAF members still did not fully accept her, she was an outlaw in the eyes of the police. Her signature was on the message sent to the police claiming responsibility for the attack. She fled deeper and deeper into the terrorist life. From December 1978 to February 1979, she attended a training camp for PLO terrorists in South Yemen in the company of other RAF members. A few months later, she insisted on taking part in an attempt to assassinate Alexander Haig, then head of NATO, in Belgium. It was Albrecht who took the bomb material to the town where Haig was visiting, where, in a nearby apartment hideout, she awaited the RAF bombers. That attempt ultimately failed.

Not long after, Albrecht fled to East Germany, where she took up her new life, never telling her new husband about her past life. Had the Berlin Wall not crumbled, she and quite a few of her cohorts might have lived quietly ever after. But Albrecht, who now goes by her husband's last name, Becker, told the judge she felt relieved to have been caught. She was repentant and hoped to put her terrorist past behind her once and for all. The judge sentenced her to twelve years, a relatively lenient sentence. One can't help wondering whether conditions under the East German communist regime might have helped change her mind.

At the outset, the Red Army Faction terrorist group was not preoccupied with German business executives as a prime target. The seeds of the group were sown in 1968, when Andreas Baader and Gudrun Ensslin set fire to two department stores in Frankfurt to protest the Vietnam War. From that act they graduated to bombing American military installations, before the core of the gang—Baader, Ensslin, Ulrike Meinhof and two others—were caught by the police. Other members followed with a series of attacks in an attempt to have the jailed members freed. In April 1975 the German embassy in Stockholm was occupied; the terrorists detonated a bomb after the German government refused to meet their demands. Four people were killed, including two members of the RAF itself.

In July 1977 came the Ponto affair. Two months after the kidnapping attempt failed, the RAF kidnapped Hanns Martin Schleyer, a member of the management board of Daimler-Benz as well as the head of the BDI. This kidnapping took place right in the streets of Cologne: the terrorists forced Schleyer's car off to the side of the street and opened fire with machine guns. Schleyer's driver and three of Schleyer's guards in a trailing car were killed. Again the RAF demanded the release of their jailed comrades. Again the German government refused. Matters escalated a week later when a Lufthansa jet was hijacked in Mallorca by Palestinian terrorists and taken to Mogadishu in Somalia. There German special forces raided the plane, freeing ninety-one hostages. A few hours later, Baader, Ensslin and another jailed RAF colleague committed suicide (Ulrike Meinhof had already done the honors back in May 1975). Hanns Martin Schleyer's corpse was found in the trunk of a Mercedes in France, just over the German border.

The core of the gang was gone, but the killing continued, and more and more often the targets were businessmen. In February 1985 the head of the Motoren- und Turbinen-Union, Ernst Zimmermann, was shot. MTU, since acquired by Daimler-Benz, produced engines for Germany's Leopard tanks. A little over a year after the Zimmermann murder, Siemens managing board member Karl Heinz Beckurts was blown up in his car by a bomb at the side of the road. The bomb and detonation system were quite sophisticated: an optical beam crossing the road was switched on by a radio control and then triggered when the car went past. The same kind of bomb would kill Alfred Herrhausen, the head of Deutsche Bank, in November 1989.

The murder of Herrhausen, coming only three weeks after the first crack in the Berlin Wall, sent out a particularly ominous signal. The RAF founders were long since dead, the Reds on the other side of the rusted-out Iron Curtain were dying a symbolic death, but the remnants of the RAF were still at it, conducting a reign of terror against German business. The RAF claims to be fighting against the capitalist system, but it might as well throw in the towel. The day Herrhausen was killed, Deutsche Bank's stock closed up a few points on the Frankfurt exchange. The market's early euphoria over the opening of the Berlin Wall was still going strong. The Red Army Faction sold German business short—and lost.

The roundup of a number of RAF members in East Germany in June 1990, combined with the collapse of the East German government—which had supported the terrorist activities— seemed like the end of the RAF. Yet despite the German police's best efforts, a hard-core RAF contingent remains armed and dangerous. In April 1991, an RAF sniper perched in a tree on a quiet Düsseldorf street shot and killed Detlev Rohwedder in the bedroom of his home. For years the CEO of the Hoesch steel company, Rohwedder had just taken over as head of the Treuhandanstalt, the agency charged with privatizing East German businesses.

The identities of the RAF's current ringleaders and the number of members who remain active is a mystery. The RAF does not hold a general assembly and take motions from the floor. Members use code names and, depending on their status within the organization, are privy to varying degrees of information. The underground communication channels are extensive, as even jailed members are kept abreast of goings-on outside the prison walls. There is even speculation that certain prisoners may be calling the shots. The difficulty of finding members still on the loose is compounded by their tendency to appear outwardly like everyday members of society. Jailed members include a music teacher, a nurse, a taxi driver, an electrician. Many of them received their baccalaureate and attended a university, if only to drop out later.

The RAF still has many hangers-on who aren't necessarily active members, as was evident at the trial of Susanne Albrecht. When recalcitrant witnesses such as Brigitte Mohnhaupt or Christian Klar were brought in—all of whom, incidentally, did little more than spout militant rhetoric during the trial—more than 150 onlookers applauded and cheered their heroes. Conversely, the jailed witnesses who had renounced their RAF past were loudly jeered by the sympathizers. Such acolytes present a problem for the police and the businessmen: are they merely deluded, harmless onlookers, or are they potential recruits in this organized campaign of violence?

With RAF zealots still on the loose, German businessmen have a lot more to worry about than meeting the next quarterly earnings forecast. Italian businessmen had to worry about the Red Brigades during the 1970s, and the French contended with Action Directe in the 1980s, but both these groups were completely dismantled by the police. The Irish Republican Army has targeted British political figures and largely left British executives alone. In the United States, few executives ever stop to think about terrorism. For them the main challenge consists only of insulating themselves from the random street violence that plagues so many American cities. That can be as easy as moving to the suburbs.

For all the danger that goes along with a high-profile executive career, however, most German executives take a somewhat fatalistic view of terrorism. Yes, they worry less about the length of their stretch limousine and more about the thickness of its armor plating. Yes, they work behind bulletproof glass in their offices. Some even have several bodyguards. Still, as Ulrich Cartellieri of the Deutsche Bank management board puts it, "If they want to get you, they will get you."

Cartellieri and many German businessmen also seem to think that the problem of RAF terrorism could be solved more rapidly if law enforcement officials were not held back by strict privacy laws. As it is, phone wiretapping and cross-indexing of government files on individuals is strictly curtailed under German law. No one wants another Nazi police state. Nevertheless, one can understand the irritation of many executives when the same left-wing politicians who had opposed a more liberal use of wiretapping to fight terrorism suddenly took up the cause of corporate wiretapping in the wake of revelations of illegal exports to countries like Libya and Iraq. (Ultimately, legislation that would have allowed corporate wiretaps was defeated.)

Is it fair to say that the German executive "pays" for his well-being in the form of the daily threat of terrorism? Not really. The spate of terrorist attacks in Germany over the last twenty years seems to have abated somewhat. In May 1992 the RAF even signaled a willingness to halt its activities. As constricted as executive life in Germany may appear to Americans, all in all it's not a bad deal.

PART THREE

THE FUTURE OF GERMAN BUSINESS

"Since everything is being built from scratch, in several years the region will be one of the most productive in the world. Entrepreneurs investing in eastern Germany for the cheap labor had better stay home. With the right training, the Germans in the East will rapidly close the productivity gap with the West and earn comparable wages. The Americans, English, French are making a mistake by not setting up production in [eastern Germany]."

—REINER PILZ

10

The Burden of the Past: Forced Labor, Arms Sales and Other Crimes

The headlines screamed out the awful fact—secret chemical weapons sales to the Iraqis—for all the world to read just months before the start of the 1991 Gulf War, in which American and other allied forces—but no Germans—routed the Iraqi army from Kuwait. Only a year earlier, similar headlines announced that chemical plants had been shipped from Germany to Libya. On both occasions, a handful of Mittelstand companies and some lax governmental supervision had succeeded in crippling the world-wide image of German business in the few electronic seconds it takes for news to travel around the globe. Where once people had thought of quality and efficiency, suddenly they thought of amorality and greed and—worst of all—the Holocaust.

Try as the Germans might to atone for their dark past, all it takes is a few missteps for the specter of the Holocaust to raise its ugly head once again. With the revelations about German chemical plants in Iraq and Libya, people everywhere raised an all-too-familiar question: "What's wrong with Germany?" The logic is inevitable: gassing millions of Jews and other "undesirables" at Auschwitz and Treblinka apparently wasn't enough for the Germans; German businessmen seem to be picking up where Hitler left off. Unscrupulously, remorselessly, shamelessly, German capitalists have provided Arab tyrants like Moamar Khaddafi of Libya and Saddam Hussein of Iraq the means to produce poison gas to kill more Jews or Kurds—even Americans. The motive? Mere profit. Never mind that the German-built plants had been built, ostensibly, to produce pesticides. The heavy antiaircraft guns surrounding the factories at Samarra in Iraq and Rabita in Libya left little doubt as to the true purpose of the plants. Later revelations linked German companies to Iraqi attempts to build an atomic bomb.

A similar logic pervades another extremely sensitive issue in German business circles: the plight of the millions of people forced to labor for the Third Reich's war effort. Virtually all of the major German corporations used foreign civilians as forced labor during the war: Volkswagen, Siemens, BMW, Daimler-Benz, AEG (now part of Daimler-Benz), Rheinmetall, Krupp, Klöckner, IG Farben (now split into BASF, Hoechst and Bayer) and many, many others. This dark episode in German corporate history is still a smoldering issue, as the surviving victims of the forced labor pursue a long, lonely quest for recognition.

As a nation, Germany will never be severed entirely from its brutal, terrifying past. Yet the extent to which the sins of the father have been visited upon the sons whenever such sensitive issues arise seems unfair to many Germans. What more can they do to live down that past? It's an important question for Germany in general and German business in particular: at stake is not only their reputation, but continuing success in world markets as well.

Sleeping with the Enemy

Like the Holocaust itself, the highly emotional subject of chemical weapons cannot help but bring out the worst in everyone. The Germans themselves developed mustard gas, the first chemical weapon, during World War I; its use by both sides cost nearly 20,000 soldiers their lives and over 1 million their health. Death by mustard gas, which breaks down a person's immune system, was considered so grisly and unsportsmanlike—compared to bleeding to death from bayonet, bullet or shrapnel wounds—that an international convention was drafted in 1925 prohibiting the use of chemical weapons. Since that time, the world's diplomats have done their best to limit chemical weapons, albeit with mixed results. In the late 1930s, German scientists working for IG Farben developed nerve gas, which the Nazis used as well as hydrogen cyanide as part of their "final solution." Other, more limited uses of chemical weapons have occurred since World War II, most recently by Saddam Hussein in 1987 against Kurds in northern Iraq and against the Iranian Army during their eight-year war. The nerve gas Hussein used was presumably produced in Iraq with German machinery.

Given the invariably strong reactions toward both the Holocaust and chemical weapons, the worldwide condemnation of Germany following the exposure of its role in the Iraqi and Libyan weapons plants was inevitable. Nevertheless, most Germans, while clearly embarrassed, saw matters slightly differently.

Why, Germans asked, should the Holocaust always be dragged out of the closet on such occasions? Why should the government's failure to intervene in a handful of recent Middle Eastern deals immediately be construed as a return on the part of Germany to an anti-Semitic, fascist state? Why doesn't anyone ever mention the nineteen other countries, including the Soviet Union, France and the United States, that provided Iraq with far more military hardware during the 1980s than Germany did? What about the various companies from Italy, the Netherlands, France and the United States that supplied components for those same chemical weapons plants? Shouldn't such exports be controlled through international cooperation? At any rate, the German firms involved were hardly representative of German industry as a whole. The shipments to Iraq involved a subsidiary of Karl Kolb GmbH and the now defunct Water Engineering Trading GmbH; in Libya, the culprit was Imhausen-Chemie GmbH. All belonged to the Mittelstand; none were household names.

The Germans have conceded that the pervasive moral corruption in Germany during the Third Reich created an atmosphere that tolerated—even promoted—business crimes like forced labor or the knowing production of hydrogen cyanide for the death camps. Today, however, Germany has solid democratic institutions, and business in general is run just as ethically as it is in any highly industrialized nation. No one denies that the shipments to Iraq and Libya were unethical. But does anyone really think that the suppliers of conventional weapons to such countries operate on a higher moral plane? The laws governing German weapons exports are generally far more restrictive than those in the United States or other European countries. Unfortunately, the Germans only belatedly got around to controlling "dual-use," that is, civilian and military, facilities like chemical plants and nuclear technology.

A chemical plant waiting to be shipped doesn't look terribly threatening: some pumps, pipes, storage tanks, electronic control instruments and the like. And because the chemicals used in pesticide production and nerve gas production are virtually identical, a factory's true function is not always evident until it is actually built. Only subtle differences, like the size of the ventilation system or the absence of a centrifuge, can tip off an investigator. Controlling chemical plant exports demands a great deal of technical expertise.

Be that as it may, there is more to the story. The problem, in part, was philosophical. Before 1984, German law prohibited exports of dual-use goods only if built expressly to produce weaponry. That's not much of a constraint in a highly technological world where such distinctions can be tragically unclear. In 1984 the law was modified to prohibit the export without governmental authorization of equipment capable of being made suitable for military purposes. Yet at the same time, the German agency in charge of supervising such exports, the Bundesamt für Wirtschaft

(BAW), was sadly understaffed: throughout the 1980s, only some six people were responsible for supervising all exports involving potentially sensitive chemical or nuclear technology. It would seem that the world's leading export nation was far more concerned with moving the merchandise than with inspecting it.

Two veteran reporters for the German weekly *Der Spiegel*, Hans Leyendecker and Richard Rickelmann, followed the trail of German exports to the Middle East. Their account, outlined in a short book, makes it abundantly clear that the German government ignored repeated warnings of German wrongdoing.

As early as 1982, the German embassy in Baghdad had been tipped off that the Iraqis were planning to manufacture chemical weapons in Samarra, some sixty miles to the north of Baghdad. Two years later the CIA presented German government officials with evidence that nerve gas was indeed being produced in Samarra—and with German technology. German inspectors were dispatched to Samarra to investigate a plant built by a subsidiary of Karl Kolb GmbH, but Kolb officials and the Iraqis never showed the inspectors the entire facility. The investigators' conclusion: the plant was not outfitted for weapons production.

The Iraqis had also contracted for Water Engineering Trading GmbH of Hamburg to build a nerve gas facility in Al-Falluja, some forty miles west of Baghdad. That plant was built in 1986, but only in August 1990 did the Germans get sufficient proof to arrest the company's principals. Both the Karl Kolb and WET cases are pending in court.

In the Libya case, Imhausen-Chemie GmbH made the government's task more difficult by covering its tracks with remarkable care. The nerve gas plant was officially destined for Hong Kong, and the German government ignored warnings sent from its Moscow embassy in 1985 that it was in fact bound for Libya. In October 1988 United States intelligence officials informed their German counterparts of the German connection in the desert sands of Rabita, but again the German government stalled. Chancellor Helmut Kohl, refusing to believe the allegations, went so far as to criticize openly the American claims as lacking in concrete proof. When auditors from the German finance ministry were sent to look over the Imhausen books in January 1989, they found invoices, travel receipts to and from Hong Kong and even photographs of a plant under construction amid green hills and fields with Chinese workers clearly visible. At a press conference in January 1989, the government auditors openly vouched for the company head, Jürgen Hippenstiel-Imhausen. A few weeks later, the German police, following other leads, uncovered the deception. Hippenstiel-Imhausen was sentenced to only five years in jail for illegal exports.

The three firms mentioned, Karl Kolb, Water Engineering (since gone bankrupt) and Imhausen-Chemie, were the main offenders. There were other companies involved to a lesser degree either as subcontractors or in other capacities. Still, a wholesale indictment of German business in the wake of these scandals would be a gross exaggeration. Several German companies, approached by the Iraqis or other middlemen, declined to do the dirty business. The German government never made a priority of controlling illegal exports, and even ethical businessmen failed to see the need for stricter monitoring.

Have the gas plant scandals caused the Germans to rethink their export policy? The question remains open. Hans Leyendecker of *Der Spiegel* remains cautious about any significant change in the German export philosophy: "The concern with business ethics typically stopped at the border. What happened beyond there was always someone else's problem. I thought that with the poison gas scandals that attitude would at last change, but I'm not so sure. Once the debates blow over it may well be back to business as usual." Indeed, the Germans sometimes seem more anxious to prevent a chief executive from flying in a company jet on personal business than in stopping an illegal export that could cost thousands or millions of people their lives.

Legislation that would have allowed the government to wiretap company phones and search company mail was narrowly defeated in the German legislature. The BAW, charged with overseeing exports, saw its resources and manpower close to tripled. Major business and trade associations such as the Bundesverband der Deutschen Industrie (BDI) and the Deutscher Industrie- und Handelstag (DIHT) agreed to help disseminate information on illicit attempts to procure weaponry or other dual-use technology.

In terms of a change in export philosophy, though, the position taken by Edzard Reuter, chief executive of Daimler-Benz, is revealing. Both before and after the January 1991 Gulf War, the media frenzy over the poison gas scandals spilled over to leading German blue-chip firms. These companies drew fire for furnishing Iraq with weapons, even though the transactions were legal. Daimler-Benz, through its connection with the recently acquired arms manufacturer Messerschmitt-Bölkow-Blohm, naturally drew a lot of fire for supplying Iraq indirectly with helicopters, and with antitank missiles and launchers through MBB's French joint venture subsidiary. Quoted in an April 1991 issue of *Die Zeit,* an influential German weekly paper, Reuter argued that military exports should be prohibited to those countries where even "the slightest doubt as to their trustworthiness" exists. At the same time, MBB was pursuing sales of Tornado fighter planes to South Korea and rocket technology to India.

The Undying Issue of Forced Labor

During the Nazi era, German businessmen more or less had to collaborate with the Nazis just to stay in business. Of course, some collaborated with more zeal than others, and after the war the most zealous of the lot were tried as war criminals. The coal and steel barons who supplied the Wehrmacht, men like Friedrich Flick and Alfried Krupp, were sentenced to jail and the payment of heavy fines. Some thirty-two directors of IG Farben, makers of the gas that killed the Jews, were also given jail sentences. Yet collaboration between business and the Nazis was even more widespread than the criminal record indicates, and nowhere is this more true than in the more or less secret history of forced labor.

The total number of forced laborers working for German companies during the war reached almost 10 million, of which some 6.5 million were foreign civilians, 2.5 million were prisoners of war and over 150,000 were from the concentration camps. In the early war years, foreign labor was "recruited" from occupied countries like France, Poland and Holland. Forbidden to mingle with the German population, such laborers had to live in special camps. Conditions in these camps varied, with Russians, Poles and other Slavs treated far worse than, say, French or Danish workers. The demand for foreign labor at the beginning of the war was mostly agricultural. Only when the German invasion of the Soviet Union bogged down on the way to Moscow did private firms realize that their regular German labor force would be busy at the front. Maintaining production meant tapping all the pools of slave labor. More and more foreign civilians who could not be recruited to work in Germany were rounded up and deported to work in German factories. Not since the end of slavery in America had so many people been put to work against their will.

Contrary to popular belief, concentration camp inmates were in reality but a minute part of the forced labor equation, and for the most part they were put to work toward the end of the war when the Germans became desperate.

One oft-heard defense of the private companies that employed the concentration camp inmates is that the inmates' chances of survival increased by working for the companies. This argument is at best a partial truth. To be sure, the wretched physical condition of the slave laborers was a drag on productivity, and some firms did try to improve it with a few extra rations of food. Some companies, like BMW, even went so far as to impart a few skills to the laborers, although a comparison here with the centuries-old apprenticeship system would be farfetched, to say the least. Work in the factories was no picnic, and depending on the company, the foremen could be just as harsh as the SS, which did not always have the manpower to watch the slaves.

Worse than any cruel foreman, though, was the overall labor equation, since the workers employed inside the plants accounted for only one half of the total. The other half consisted of the builders. For companies to gain access to the labor, they had to have production sites close by. Also, the threat that Allied bombing might disrupt production meant that underground plants had to be built. The work was grueling, and the average life span of a construction worker was only a few weeks. Although the private companies themselves seldom built such bunkers—that job was often left to the SS—company executives were perfectly well aware of what was going on. At one site near the Bavarian town of Mühldorf am Inn, leading executives from AEG, Siemens and Rheinmetall met in December 1944 to see how construction of the Weingut bunker, where some forty-two companies were slated to build production facilities, was proceeding. Particularly revealing is that the meeting took place at a time when it had become clear that Germany would lose the war. It seemed that the industrialists' primary concern was not continuing production but rather saving some precious capital for after the war. Of the 9,000 forced laborers who toiled to build the Weingut bunker, over a third died.

The German executives who took over after 1945 quite naturally agreed with the concept that German firms had acted as "agents" of the Third Reich, and as such had hardly been capable of making decisions independently. This attitude, held by the German government as well as Allied governments eager to see Germany assume the Third Reich's former debts, absolved in one bold stroke all German companies from any individual liability concerning forced labor. On more than one occasion, the agency principle was upheld in German courts. No wonder, then, that German executives today consider the chapter of collaboration with the Nazis—and the forced labor it involved—to be closed. In this view, reparations have been paid to the surviving victims wherever possible, German companies have acted ethically since the war and they should now be allowed to get on with business without the attendant negative publicity.

In the early postwar years, to lump German companies together as mere agents of the Reich was politically expedient. At the 1952 London debt conference, where West Germany agreed to assume DM 7.3 billion in pre- and postwar debts, the issue of individual claims against German companies was deferred. It was thought at the time that such claims would only jeopardize the German government's ability to repay all that debt. Every mark paid to an individual meant one less that could be used for debt repayment, and in the early 1950s no one could know that West Germany would become an economic powerhouse in the coming decades. Once Germany was on its feet economically, though, this justification for the agency defense was gone. Moreover, the historical record clearly shows that private companies were not entirely tools of the Nazis and that they acted with independence.

Just as revelations about the conduct of many German companies during the war have discredited the agency theory, so too did several anomalies after the war. Concurrent with the 1952

London debt conference, several leading Jewish groups—known collectively as the Claims Conference—in company with the State of Israel negotiated reparations with the German government. Germany was not legally obligated to Israel or the Jewish groups, but the moral obligation was tremendous. Germany's chancellor, Konrad Adenauer, agreed that Germany would give Israel DM 3 billion and the other Jewish groups DM 450 million—this at a time when Germany's future economic power was by no means assured. Meanwhile, thanks to the efforts of Benjamin Ferencz, the Jewish delegation succeeded in getting additional reparations money from six private firms—including Siemens, Krupp and Telefunken-AEG (today part of Daimler-Benz). Thus, while private companies such as Siemens felt obligated to compensate Jewish victims, there was no such obligation toward its forced laborers.

Waltraud Blass was one of those forced laborers. In 1990, at the ripe old age of seventy, she brought a suit against Siemens AG for around DM 85,000 in back pay, unpaid pension and damages for her pain and suffering. Blass's story is a bit atypical in that she was German, whereas the overwhelming majority of forced laborers were foreigners. Her case nevertheless shows how the German legal system works against private claims against individual companies. Her parents had been active in the German Communist party during the rise of the Nazis, and she was taken to court with them in March 1943. On her way out of the courthouse in Wuppertal, she was grabbed by the Gestapo and sent to the Ravensbrück concentration camp not far from Berlin. At Ravensbrück, Blass was selected to work in the nearby Siemens factory, where she spent ten months.

After the war, Blass was eligible for reparations from the German government—DM 5 for every day she had spent in Ravensbrück. Siemens, however, never paid her for the twelve-hour workdays she had put in at the Siemens factory. The German legislature's 1953 law governing compensation for German victims of the Nazis made no provision for forced labor, and the early jurisprudence clearly favored the agency principle. It wasn't for another forty-odd years that Blass was persuaded to sue for compensation. Her lawyers, who conceded they were using her case as a test, argued that the agency defense had become discredited as time passed.

Waltraud Blass lost her case against Siemens well before it came to trial on the grounds that the statute of limitations had run out—she would have had to sue within three years of the 1953 legislation. Her case had been supported by Aktion Sühnezeichen Friedensdienste, a private association seeking, in the words of member Thomas Lutz, to redress past injustices. As Lutz pointed out, "The cost of an appeal was prohibitive and the chances of reversing the outcome were slim, but the publicity we got was a partial success."

Lutz's organization is not the only one working on behalf of forced labor victims. But for these various organizations, getting a small write-up in the paper is often the only tangible success. What irks the victims above all is the way in which their cause has been quietly swept under the rug by the German government and by private companies. Whereas after the war the German government and several Germans themselves felt an obligation to help out Jewish victims and Israel, other forced labor victims never received any such consideration.

Hermann Langbein, a survivor of Auschwitz, heads an organization dedicated to getting reparations from private companies. He points out in an article published in 1989 that most German companies have succeeded in hiding behind legal loopholes over the years to avoid responsibility for the forced labor of the war years. Some examples: In 1969, after trying to get executives at Daimler-Benz to acknowledge the company's debt to its forced laborers during the war, Langbein's organization received a letter to the effect that Daimler-Benz AG had not used any forced labor from concentration camps. When Daimler was presented with evidence to the contrary, the company concocted a response that the forced laborers had in fact been employed by the Daimler-Benz Motorenbau GmbH, a subsidiary. How's that for splitting hairs? Only in June 1988 did Daimler-Benz announce that it was creating a DM 20 million foundation to help compensate for the company's onetime forced laborers. How the money will reach the individual victims is not clear, but Daimler's effort is certainly a step in the right direction.

While other German companies, notably Volkswagen, have agreed to create a foundation for victims, an overwhelming majority of German companies have opted to bury the issue. When Langbein's organization presented the case for compensation to executives at BMW, the initial answer (in 1969) was much the same as Daimler's initial response: a stout denial of the use of forced labor during the war. Besides, went the response, the statute of limitations has run out on such cases anyway. When BMW was presented with proof that prisoners from Dachau had in fact been slave laborers at the BMW-Allach plant outside of Munich, the firm's response was—strangely enough—that the Allach plant was part of the BMW Triebwerkebau GmbH, a subsidiary. To this day BMW has done nothing else.

Daimler-Benz and BMW have been singled out here, but the response is almost always the same from all the companies involved. Today, when these companies give out a published history of their firm for public relations purposes, the narrative predictably stops around 1939. Usually words like "then came the war, where 80% of the company's factories were bombed" suffice to cover the six-year interlude up until 1945. Then the narrative resumes with the heroic effort to rebuild described in great detail. Naturally, a company has a right to put its best foot forward, but one could hope for a slightly more objective assessment, a "mea culpa," and some expression of the firm's intention never to let such an incident happen again.

Of course the brush-off is not always based on conspiratorial intent. In many cases, company executives today simply do not know the detailed history of forced labor under the Third Reich, nor how the matter was dealt with after the war. The German government decided the issue had been settled, so on with business. Furthermore, few Germans in the general public today understand the issue and are fed up with paying the debts of the Nazi past anyway. How long must the sons and daughters continue to be punished for the sins of the fathers?

In gross terms, the Germans have shelled out over DM 80 billion in reparations of various kinds, and the bill keeps rising. The biggest chunk of that money, over DM 70 billion, has gone to those victims who lived in Germany and were persecuted by the Nazis. Germany has been paying this money since the end of the war, and when the last of these victims dies, sometime after the year 2000, payments will have reached over DM 100 billion. Although the share of these reparations in the current German budget is relatively small—around 1 percent—the cost in relative terms was much greater in earlier decades, as much as 5 percent of the budgets of the day.

Germany also paid out the aforementioned DM 3.45 billion to Israel and the Claims Conference, as well as an additional DM 1 billion to be split among twelve mostly Western European governments. This latter billion was agreed to in 1956 as a sort of bone to be thrown to countries such as France and England, which had also been victimized by the Nazis; individual claimants from these countries had to address their own governments for compensation. However, countries such as Poland, Czechoslovakia and the Soviet Union—with which West Germany did not maintain diplomatic relations—were not covered by these payments. (The Soviets took compensation in kind immediately after the war by dismantling factories in eastern Germany and shipping them back to the USSR.)

The case of Poland illustrates how the German government has continued to help private industry avoid paying compensation. In the 1950s and '60s, the government reaction was blunt: no peace treaty, no reparations. The logic of the cold war dictated that compensation money should not go toward helping the enemy. After Germany and Poland signed a "normalization" treaty in 1970, Germany gave Poland a DM 1 billion loan with a preferred interest rate in the belief that this generosity would settle all Polish claims. The Poles, however, continued to press Germany to recognize the individual claims of forced laborers. Then came German reunification in 1990, and the claims issue became even more entangled. When the German government seemed unwilling to sign a treaty cementing the postwar boundary between the two countries, the international press condemned the delay, and there was speculation that perhaps the Germans did in fact harbor notions of recouping the prewar eastern territories ceded to Poland after the war.

In fact, Germany's real objective was to get the Polish government to drop the compensation claims on behalf of its citizens. Ultimately, a compromise was reached. A German-Polish "friendship treaty" signed in June 1991 skirted the issue of compensation, but four months later the two countries announced the creation of a DM 500 million foundation to compensate former victims. Similar negotiations are under way between Germany and Czechoslovakia. These developments are welcome news for those remaining forced labor victims, today perhaps 2 to 3 million strong, who were previously denied any kind of compensation. German companies no doubt welcome the news, since they can claim to be off the financial hook definitively. Whether that lets them off the moral hook is another matter entirely.

While academics, lawyers and the victims of forced labor themselves ponder the legal and moral obligation of German companies, the money crowd in Frankfurt, London and Wall Street is more concerned with—what else?—money. A typical concern: if German companies decide to back up their moral obligation to forced labor victims with cash, how much might such compensation affect company earnings? The answer depends on the numbers used. Waltraud Blass sued Siemens for DM 85,000; multiply that benchmark figure by 2 million unpaid forced laborers still alive, and the overall figures for German industry rapidly escalate into the hundreds of billions. But the Blass case was intended as a symbol—and was unsuccessful. The victims and their representatives would probably be content with far smaller sums. Daimler-Benz's DM 20 million payment, which represents just over 1 percent of 1990 earnings, has sufficed to quiet many of Daimler's ex–forced laborers.

Ultimately, the refusal by many German companies to compensate their onetime forced laborers in some form raises a perplexing question: how can these companies be so socially minded on the one hand—what with apprenticeship training, job benefits and so on—yet on the other be so indifferent to the claims of people who suffered so much? There is no simple answer. Daimler-Benz and Volkswagen made a belated effort, and continued pressure on the others may bring more results. If it's any consolation, Germans have made more of an effort to come to grips with the issue than, say, the Japanese. During the war, Japanese firms used millions of Koreans and other Asians as forced laborers, but today nary a peep is heard in Japan on the matter. Ulrich Herbert, a professor at the University of Hagen who has written extensively on the issue of forced labor in Germany, says, "I gave a speech on the subject in Japan once and was met with the most dumbfounded silence. There they have not even begun to recognize the issue."

People looking for reasons to criticize German business can always point to the failure of some companies to make up for their wartime abuses of forced labor or to other firms for thinking only of profits in providing Middle East tyrants with equipment for mass destruction. On the other hand, these problems have more to do with business per se than with anything particularly German. The Nazi period was not, as Marxists like to portray it, a natural outgrowth of capitalism or the work of some powerful industrialists. National Socialism came, and German business adapted. Nor should all of German business be blamed for the crime of a few illegal export deals, nefarious as those exports may have been. The export philosophy for dual-use goods was too lax, and German business must take its share of blame for not having recognized the problem, but to focus too much on Germany is to ignore the failures of other countries as well.

11

The Lost Country: East Germany

Siegfried Sack sits staring at the Spree. The river flows through the heart of Berlin with the eternal strength of all rivers, while the world of the fifty-nine-year-old Sack and his fellow ex–East Germans is crashing to a halt. "I'm afraid socialism came to this world a few centuries too early, and it was done wrong," says Sack regretfully.

Sack is a large but unassuming man, the kind of professor you would gladly drink beer with in a pub after class, discussing the issues of the day. But in July 1991, one year after German currency reform and eight months after he lost his job, Sack has other worries. He is caught between decreasing benefits and rising costs. In a few months he will fall into the category of the officially unemployed, and his government benefits will decrease to just over DM 1,000 a month. The rent on his apartment will jump from DM 109 to DM 513 a month. The cost of electricity will go up, as will the phone, the subway, who knows what else?

Sack, who is approaching retirement age, was never given the chance to save up for retirement in a capitalist economy. Sack might easily be on the verge of despair, but he is determined to educate himself further, to learn the workings of a free market, and—he hopes—to teach it to others. Still, he needs a job. "I would sell the *Bild Zeitung* [Germany's conservative daily rabble sheet] in the street if I could, even though I don't agree with what's inside," says Sack. "The problem is, all the jobs, all of them, are taken—garbageman, you name it."

The Present Lives Up to the Past

That East Germany was an economic failure is no secret. Germans who lived there, like Sack, know that better than anyone. But East Germany was more than a failed economic system; it was also a country with its own identity. Most people in the West know only the dark side: the Soviet client state that built the Berlin Wall and shot its own citizens who tried to flee; the state that trained terrorists throughout the world (including the Red Army Faction, which operated next door); the government that lined its own pockets with perks and privileges while the rest of the population found itself too frequently deprived of even the bare essentials of life.

The only favorable recognition East Germany received in the international arena centered on its spectacular Olympic sports program, and even that had a dark side. Despite the country's minuscule size and population compared to the United States or the USSR, East Germany regularly ranked alongside the two superpowers in Olympic medal counts. But as the all-too-masculine appearance of East German female swimmers suggested—and as East German sports authorities have since confirmed—success in the East German sports programs was spelled s-t-e-r-o-i-d. Of course, that was never East Germany's problem alone.

The image visitors came away with when East Germany

opened its borders to Westerners in late 1989 and early 1990 was
bleak indeed. Werner Otto described it as "magical," but he was
referring to the feeling that visiting the country was like stepping
back in time. That's fine for an observer on a day trip, but the
people who live there might find a step forward into the modern
world somewhat more desirable. Those steps are just beginning.

Dilapidated apartment buildings and factories stand alongside
long rows of drab public buildings. Everything new seems to be
made out of concrete. For many citizens, hot running water is not
a given. The government managed to keep some old showpiece
buildings in the center of East Berlin—Humboldt University, the
Opera—in modest shape. But much of the finest baroque archi-
tecture in Dresden, which was heavily bombed by the British and
Americans at the end of the war, has not been restored and remains black with soot.

The car that East Germans used to wait years to buy, the
Trabant, is a joke by Western standards: tinny and quick to break
down, it is also an environmental nightmare, emitting thick
clouds of noxious smoke from the oil-and-gasoline mixture it
burns.

Cars are not the only polluters. East German electric power
comes almost exclusively from brown coal, the country's only
energy resource. But self-sufficiency makes for a very dirty sky.
The vast, decayed chemical factories at Bitterfeld and Leuna used
to employ more than 50,000 workers, but, thanks to the toxic
emissions, the average life span of workers and town residents
alike is woefully short. Children from these towns were sent to
summer camps on islands in the North Sea just to give them a
taste of fresh air.

The two functioning nuclear power plants were shut down
right after reunification because, built on the Chernobyl model,
they were too dangerous to operate. Yet in the southern forests
of Saxony and Thüringen, the Wismut mining company piled up
whole mountains of ore heavily laden with uranium from a
nearby mine. Nothing prevents the wind from blowing radioac-
tive dust particles into nearby towns. The East German government even allowed paving companies to use some of this rock in
road asphalt.

In the old East German factories, the machinery is fit for the junkyard, or at the very best the museum. The *Frankfurter Allge-meine Zeitung* recently ran a magazine article about the West German museum association's campaign to save many of these precious relics of an earlier industrial age before they are scrapped. At the Leuna chemical factory sat one of the last *Kreislaufgas-Umlaufpumpen,* used to synthesize ammonia. The steam-powered electric engine for the machine was built by the MAN company in 1916–17. Meanwhile, in the old Maxhütte steel factory near Saalfeld lies Europe's last Thomasstahlwerk. The outmoded steel factory is too big for a museum, but certainly the last *"Thomas-birne,"* the pear-shaped vat in which the steel was heated, would make a worthy museum piece.

With East Germany's record of dubious accomplishments, it's hard to understand how the people could put up with such dreadful conditions for so long, let alone support the system. A partial explanation lies in the country's history. In the early years following the Second World War, no East German state was going to be formed without Stalin's approval. But the state that was formed, the German Democratic Republic, was not entirely a Soviet puppet state. There were Germans after the war who, in the tradition of Marx, Engels and Rosa Luxemburg—who was executed for her role in the leftist Berlin uprisings of 1919—wanted to establish communism in Germany. There were also those who thought that, given the recent catastrophic experience with fascism, socialism might indeed be worth a try. Bertolt Brecht, for one, chose to cast his lot with the East, although he died in 1956, soon after making the move to East Berlin.

For the first five or ten years, the gap in the standard of living between West and East Germany was not that noticeable. Even when the gap began to widen, many East Germans consoled themselves with the belief that they were working for social progress. East German women, for example, worked under better conditions than their counterparts in the West: 85 percent of East German women worked compared to fewer than 50 percent in West Germany—and the government provided day care for children.

In any case, the party line in the East parroted Marx's concept of historical materialism: all societies were headed toward social-ism. If living conditions in the West were better, the situation was only temporary. Eventually the capitalist countries would crum-ble and be replaced by socialist society. And East Germany did offer some avenues for promotion, for getting a car or a phone. Believers in the East German system concentrated more on im-proving their lot than on fretting about the capitalists next door.

East Germany also adopted much of German culture as its own, conveniently twisting Goethe and Schiller into "revolution-ary" authors who stood for social progress. Contemporary East German authors developed their own literature. Most of it was awful: the protagonists were typically required to find happiness within the collective society. But some of the literature stood up outside East Germany. Christa Wolf wrote *Nachdenken über Christa T.,* a moving, slightly critical description of life behind the Berlin Wall. And Stefan Heym, who had married an American and served in the U.S. Army before returning to his native Ger-many, won international recognition for his books.

In short, the feeling in East Germany after the war in many ways resembled that of Werner Otto: we survived, we can start again. A lot of East Germans sincerely thought they were work-ing to build a better world through socialism.

Siegfried Sack was fourteen when the war ended. "I was active in a sort of Hitler Youth for younger children," he says matter-of-factly. "I was glad to get a uniform. My father was a Nazi, not high up, just a town representative in a small village near the border of Czechoslovakia, but a Nazi nevertheless." After the war, Sack learned the wheelmaking trade. It took a while to re-think his beliefs and become a socialist: "I struck in 1953," he says proudly of the first major labor dissension against the East Ger-man government. But he joined the party in 1955. In the 1960s he studied economics at the University of Leipzig and began teaching there in 1969.

Sack considered Marxist doctrine a useful body of thought—*Denkwerk*—but some notions he just could not swallow. "I had problems with historical materialism [Marx's theory that societies necessarily evolve toward socialism]. I had less of a problem with dialectical materialism [the notion that society is changed through dialectical forces, usually summed up in the triad of thesis, antithesis and synthesis]." Since Sack's special field of study was capitalism—albeit through a socialist lens—his hours were not spent studying the finer points of Marxism anyway. Sack's first doctoral dissertation, completed in 1968, was about the switch from coal to oil in the West German electric industry. In 1986 he completed a second dissertation, on the changes in the economic foundations of U.S. foreign policy.

Sack visited the United States on nine different occasions. Most of the visits were for conferences, but he also spent one semester at the Johns Hopkins School of Advanced International Studies on an academic exchange program. There he met with American academics and studied the ways of American capitalism. With his direct, easygoing manner, Sack enjoyed dealing with Americans. "I always fought for détente in the pursuit of knowledge," he maintains proudly.

By the 1980s Sack had switched to the Institute for International Studies in East Berlin, where he taught economics to diplomats in training. He took the Berlin job because it offered more time for research and a bit more prestige. The pay was the same. By East German standards Sack was privileged, although his standard of living was hardly opulent. He lived with his wife and daughter in a small three-room apartment in a tall, rectangular apartment block on East Berlin's Fischerinsel. For all the trips Sack made to the United States, not once was he allowed to take his wife, much as he would have liked to. "Even if I had somehow come up with the money to pay for her trip, it would have been impossible," he says with a sigh.

Still, Sack worked within the system and accepted it. Didn't he know about his government shooting escaping citizens along the Wall? Sack equivocates somewhat. "I knew there was shooting at the Wall, as did everyone else. We all knew that if a guard yelled 'Stop' and you did not stop, you would be shot. We also knew that there was shooting on the other side."

Sack is referring to the few cases in which East German border guards were shot by West German guards—cases that were exploited in East Germany for their propaganda value, especially since the official East German version of the incidents was always less than complete. Thus every East German child learned the name of the "martyr" Peter Göring, the East German guard shot

near the Berlin Wall in 1962. What most East Germans did not
learn is that Göring and other guards were shooting at an unarmed
fourteen-year-old who was trying to escape. West German guards
had to return fire to rescue the seriously injured boy, who had
barely made it across a canal onto West German soil.

Even without knowing the ugly truth about all the border
incidents, Sack—and most of his countrymen—knew that the
Wall represented an inherent weakness in the East German state.
"But," he says, "not everyone was unhappy to see the Wall go
up. East Germans often saved up money for months or waited
even longer for some scarce good to arrive on the shelves, only to
have a West German show up with deutsche marks and take it
away."

For Sack, there were other contradictions and compromises as
well. At the institute where he taught, he was able to discuss
Western economists like Milton Friedman or Josef Schumpeter
with his colleagues freely, but getting permission to do research
at a West Berlin library for the afternoon was a major hurdle.
"The authorities thought I was going in order to read Western
propaganda, and it was never easy to convince them of my reasons for going."

Ironically, the teachings of the Western economists were, according to Sack, "interesting but not really relevant to our situation." That was then. Now the forces of what Schumpeter called
"creative destruction" are quite apparent even to Sack. The only
problem is that in eastern Germany after reunification, the destruction side of the equation is so overwhelming—which is only
natural after forty years of neglected capital investment—that
Sack and the ex–East Germans must continually remind themselves that the creation is coming.

Actually, Sack says he has known since 1987 that the East
German economy could hold out for only another two years at
most. How did he know? "I'm an economist. I can calculate," he
says defiantly. Couldn't he see what was so obvious to Western
observers—that the socialist system itself was a failure? "Perhaps
one of the problems we had in East Germany was that we were
the best of the East Bloc economies, so people were not open to
new ways."

Even when it became clear that East Germany would be swallowed up by its western counterpart, Sack refused to jump ship. He remained a member of East Germany's Communist party, rebaptized the PDS (Party of Democratic Socialism) after reunification. "I felt responsible for the German Democratic Republic and the catastrophe. I was not going to be a turncoat. We had some at the institute who tried to turn with the prevailing wind, but they were fired anyway. I also wanted to help address the interests of former East German citizens. But now the party is losing its significance: there is no way we will pass the 5 percent barrier in the 1994 elections [party representation in the German parliament requires at least 5 percent of the vote]. The only question is whether I'll still be in the party to turn out the lights after everyone has left."

Sack thought he could help East Germans make the transition to a market economy, but he was fired instead. After reunification, socialist economics professors were not in high demand, and the West German government erased the institute. On his own fate, Sack remains philosophical, although he naturally wants to find work. He is obviously disappointed that he has not heard from many former academic colleagues and acquaintances in America. "When I think of the doors I opened for them in the old days," he says, "and not without risk, either . . ."

As for the transition to a market economy, Sack is bitter. He speaks for every ex–East German when he says that it could have been accomplished more smoothly. He cites the currently high unemployment figure in what was East Germany. He talks of the increasing number of suicides. He feels the Treuhandanstalt, the government agency charged with privatizing East German companies, is dragging its heels until companies that might have been saved go bankrupt. He worries that women will suffer disproportionately as they lose the free day care facilities that enabled them to work. He complains that western Germany sees eastern Germany only as an outlet for its overwhelming production capacity. He finds some truth in the popular expression that the western Germans are as overblown as their bread rolls (eastern Germans prefer their customary smaller, less airy rolls). And he is tired of hearing the Westerners say that the Easterners have to learn to roll up their sleeves and work—when a person receives four hundred rejections, Sack points out, it takes a lot of courage to ask for the four hundred and first. When fifty-five-year-old folks sit on school benches to learn anew, does that not show a desire to learn and to work?

Sack has a message for potential investors: don't think of eastern Germany as a place to find cheap labor, but as a place with good skilled workers who want to learn. "It does not matter who owns the businesses, just so they work."

Under Western Eyes

Seen from western Germany, reunification hasn't been a picnic either. Tax increases and government resources stretched to capacity have been trying for the citizens of the West as well. But for perhaps the first time in forty years, Westerners were once again working on emotion. No sooner had the Berlin Wall been breached than West German businessmen dropped what they were doing to focus on the newly rediscovered country. Businessmen, bankers, accountants, civil servants, all gave freely of their time to help advise their long-lost brothers in the East. The feeling in West German companies was "We've got to do something there," even if "what" was unclear at first.

Naturally, the first to do something were the consumer products companies. In his comment about western companies seeing in East Germany a windfall outlet for their goods, Siegfried Sack was right on the money. There was no need for large investments, just a few extra salespeople, and the pent-up demand of the long-deprived East Germans did the rest. Laundry detergent, coffee, cigarettes, newspapers and countless other products were sold for East German marks even before the terms of the July 1, 1990, currency reform were known. Said Peter Harf of Benckiser, "We figured our break-even point at six East German marks for every deutsche mark when we began selling detergent there before the currency reform was announced." Benckiser and a lot of other early entrants cleaned up once the official exchange rate was set at the corporate rate of two to one (a one-to-one rate applied to household savings up to DM 4,000). Consumer products companies were not the only ones whose business increased dramatically.

Overall, the German economy boomed in 1990 thanks to consumption in the East. Suppliers to consumer goods companies also benefited. The newsprint producer Haindl KGaA, for example, increased production by 13 percent compared to around 3 percent in a normal good year. While most major Western countries saw growth rates stagnate or decline in the midst of a worldwide recession, Germany increased its GNP by over 4 percent. Even big-ticket items like automobiles—presumably priced too high for most eastern Germans—were selling well. Some eastern Germans landed jobs in the West and bought on credit. Others had benevolent relatives in the West. One elderly German woman riding the train home to Stuttgart proudly pulled out a set of license plates from her bag: "I bought my nephew over there a Volkswagen Passat and now I have to register the plates. He was so happy."

Western Germany's capitalist economy has had little trouble satisfying the demand for goods and services in the East. But stocking supermarket shelves with laundry detergent is easy. Attracting the massive investment that provides lots of jobs is another matter. That thankless task was given to the governmental agency charged with privatizing more than 8,000 old East German businesses, the Treuhandanstalt.

The obstacles to selling these companies were legion: the companies lacked proper balance sheets; property claims from the prewar owners discouraged potential buyers; environmental liabilities were often far worse than anyone had thought; competent managers were few and far between; and on and on.

The Treuhand was an easy target for criticism. Eastern Germans felt the agency was cruelly closing down factories that, given time and financial help, might have survived. Western investors complained that the process was too slow, and that the Treuhand's criteria for selecting among competing bidders were vague (indeed the agency did not just choose the highest bidder, but in true German social market fashion, looked at a variety of factors like job preservation, investment plans, etc.).

For the most part, however, the Treuhand made the best of a bad situation. At last count, more than 5,000 companies had been privatized. The agency's president, Birgit Breuel, announced that the main work of the Treuhand would be completed by 1994.

Yet, for all the Treuhand's success in selling off the old East

German firms, the demand for outside investment in the region remains inordinately high, and for one simple reason. The July 1990 currency reform cut the legs out from under all the local businesses.

Is There Such a Thing as an East German Entrepreneur?

After the war, West Germany was built up by self-made men and entrepreneurs like Werner Otto and countless Mittelstand owners. That is less likely to be the case in rebuilding eastern Germany. To see why, consider the stories of two men named Pilz (who are not related). Reiner Pilz fled East Germany in 1960 and founded a successful building company, which has since moved into compact disc production. He is working on a triumphant return to his native land. Eberhard Pilz, meanwhile, worked for many years as the technical director of an East German trucking company and was put in charge after reunification. He has all the smarts of an entrepreneur but few of the means, and the trucking company he manages faces liquidation.

The Transmercur GmbH headquarters in Leipzig, a kind of second city for eastern Germany, are about what you might expect. A row of indistinguishable three-story prewar buildings—all in need of repair—lines the Berliner Straße; only a gleaming new Transmercur truck (leased) in one of the courtyards signals the right driveway. Once in the courtyard, the whereabouts of E. Pilz's office have to be divined: two separate entrances and a loading dock offer no clues. Choose door number two, go up the stairs and a small sign reads "Sekretariat," the right spot. Inside, the office furniture is in Holiday Inn style, circa 1950. A clunky electric Robotron typewriter is the most modern-looking piece of office equipment in sight. Past the secretary's office in the back office is E. Pilz, in his late thirties and dressed in jeans and a short-sleeved shirt, open at the collar. (One laudable accomplishment of the old East German system was seeing through the overblown fashion ways of the West.)

The account E. Pilz gives of the history of Transmercur is fairly typical for many an East German company. Formerly the VEB (short for Volkseigener Betrieb, or "people's company") Handelstransport, the company was responsible for distributing goods, mostly food, in the region surrounding Leipzig (a radius of about thirty miles). By the time of reunification, most of the company's more than 700 trucks were at least fifteen years old— "We stopped getting new ones in the early 1980s," says E. Pilz. The failure of the planned economy to produce enough trucks forced Handelstransport into a vicious circle of improvisation just to keep the trucks moving. First the company built a garage to service the trucks and replace the spare parts. When spare parts ran out, the company put people to work repairing radiators, alternators, brakes, and so on. "We should have said 'Forget it' and refused to continue," says E. Pilz. Of course, any company head who said "Forget it" would immediately have been replaced. Under the socialist system, there were no golden parachutes. In fact, there were no parachutes at all.

Under East German rule, management was treated like *Dreck,* says E. Pilz. Since the socialist system supposedly prized the working man and woman above all, and since party bureaucrats and ideologues were necessary to lead the glorious workers' movement, company managers were caught in the middle. The manager was expected to meet the production goals of the plan but was rarely given the materials and means to do so. The manager was also virtually powerless to fire lazy employees. Then the party bureaucrats insisted on having some 33 percent of the company's work force active in the so-called *"Neuerer"* groups. These groups were supposed to be the vanguard of the workers' movement inside the factories—they would offer criticism and suggestions on how to improve production. If these groups sound a bit like the now-famous Japanese quality circles, remember that Lenin presented the idea in an earlier work. Says Pilz, "Just about all of the workers here were disillusioned and wanted nothing to do with these Neuerer groups. Besides, most of our employees are truck drivers, who are independent-minded enough as it is. The party's goal was impossible to meet."

The general disillusionment with the East German system became fairly widespread beginning in the early 1980s: "A lot of qualified people just withdrew from taking any responsibility," says E. Pilz. He himself had the opportunity to become the head of VEB Handelstransport, but he turned it down to remain technical director. "I saw what the former director had to go through in dealing with the party bureaucrats on the one hand and the employees on the other, and I thought, no way." That was not his first brush with disillusionment.

E. Pilz started out as a product of the East German system. He was born in 1953, and the famous strikes of that year were long over by the time he was growing up. He spent a lot of time in a children's home, not uncommon for kids in those days. Communist indoctrination was everywhere in school from an early age: "We learned that communism has to be. It's a law. You believe."

He started studying agronomy *(Landwirtschaft)* in 1971, and as he was one of the brighter students, there was pressure to join the party, which he did: "A lot of young people like me had our doubts, but we thought we could change the system from within. But the people in the party always had excuses for what went wrong. It was either the class enemy in the West which caused us to divert too much material to military uses, or it was something else, but it was never the people in the party."

He did his military service on the border with West Germany, a position reserved for elite troops. He even joined the infamous state police, the Stasi, in 1976. He regretted that decision soon after, however: "I was signed up for twenty-five years, but I soon wanted out. I did not like the way they watched over some people and protected others. I had read about the Nazis, and I saw too many similarities with what we were doing. I was not alone in wanting out. At least twenty percent of the people who were in did not want to be. They all tried to say they wanted to spend more time with the family, but that excuse did not work very easily. I was lucky to have a friend with contacts, and I got out after three years. That's when I came here [VEB Handelstransport]. They kept watching over me here. Still, I did not quit the party, because if I had, then they really would have pursued me."

Lying low as technical director for VEB Handelstransport, E. Pilz was responsible for the truck service centers and building projects. Only when his boss was fired in the wake of the currency reform did E. Pilz agree to take the job of company head. A few people were critical, he says, arguing that he had been at the top during the party rule and that he was still there after reunification. His response was that he was a businessman before and a businessman after. As it turns out, these complaints were the least of his problems.

Most of the newly renamed Transmercur's business was lost after reunification when new western supermarket chains opened stores in the East. The chains naturally maintained their existing delivery companies to supply the stores. Transmercur, meanwhile, was in the hands of the Treuhandanstalt, which gave Pilz the task of finding a western partner. No partner was willing to invest enough to keep the company going. Pilz took on a business consultant from Frankfurt and tried to arrange for a management buyout. He asked the banks to lend the company money, but since the company had zero for collateral, the banks said no. The land on which the company built its various depots and service centers was still held by the Treuhandanstalt, which had to ensure that no claims were brought by previous owners.

E. Pilz did not give up. He leased forty new trucks, including twenty refrigerated ones. With the newer trucks he could transport over 60 percent of the merchandise. He installed two-way radios in the trucks and the various depots—the old East German phone system was virtually nonexistent, and a modern one would take another few years to develop. He developed a computer program to help maximize efficiency. His and five other ex–East German trucking companies developed a network to provide total coverage of the area in the now-defunct country.

The problems confronting Transmercur, however, were greater than any one manager could solve. Since the currency reform had cut the legs out from under all East German industry, making local production for export virtually nonexistent, Transmercur lost another advantage. "I can make more money delivering out," says E. Pilz, "since I can set the price. But most of the business is end business, delivering merchandise from elsewhere in this region. There I have no control over the price. Even when there is local production, I can't always get the business. I heard about a local cookie factory that produced eight hundred tons per month. I drove there to offer my services, but the company had already taken on a western partner who insisted on using his own trucking company."

Then there were the regulatory problems. Transmercur had to meet the old West German standards overnight. To transport food, E. Pilz needed to get refrigerated trucks and build a refrigerated storage depot. "They just plopped forty years of laws on our heads," says E. Pilz incredulously. "I spent six months just trying to learn all the commercial law. Then there's the labor law, not to mention the whole issue of liability. What if I cannot pay all the health insurance premiums, as has happened already? Then I'm personally liable if an employee gets into an accident. My current salary is only DM 31,200 per year."

A lot has been written about how eastern Germans, after forty years of communism, have lost all sense of entrepreneurism. But when E. Pilz, a typical manager, sums up the problems he faces, the voice is that of a shackled entrepreneur: "First, the Treuhandanstalt is not working. It's not that the people there don't work hard—they come to the office early and leave late—but the system is too slow. Second, the banks don't help. Third, the government says it gives this and that, but they all just talk. Fourth, the unions come along and want the most money possible in the quickest amount of time. Fifth, the workers don't get any money and they strike.

"We should have wiped out all the companies and started from scratch," continues E. Pilz. "Instead of trying to slowly dismantle the companies, which is expensive, we should have given each businessman the opportunity to start anew and hire just the people he needed."

At last look, Transmercur had managed to lay off 600 of its 1,000 workers, but its liquidity crisis was too great and E. Pilz was looking for a way to liquidate the company. He is not worried about his future. He has already had three offers from other firms, but he knows he wants to be self-sufficient. He also intends to keep his nose clean: "I just want to do ordinary business, no under-the-table deals. Right now there is a lot of that going on, cash deals for land, for instance, and no one can keep track of it all for the time being. But the people doing these deals don't realize that in a few years, the authorities will find out and the people who made the deals will be in trouble."

Driving southwest from Leipzig, the low hills of Thüringen rise above the plain, offering an end to the monotonous landscape of the north. The towns take on more character. Penetrating into the Thüringer Wald (the large forest in the southwest corner of what was East Germany), the roads wend over tall hills thickly forested with pine. Most of the houses are well kept, with flower boxes in the windows or other touches that contrast sharply with the stark dwellings of the flatlands. In this region East Germany developed a modest tourist business, with hiking trails and an occasional little ski area consisting of a lone T-bar lift perhaps. In some of the quainter towns, there are even a few hotels and restaurants.

The town of Suhl, which lies at the end of a valley deep in these Thüringen hills, was too big to escape the communist blight entirely—a large block of ugly concrete apartments mars the landscape on one side of town. Suhl has some industry, the best known being the old sport shotgun and rifle manufacturer Suhler Jagdwaffen. In this town the onetime refugee from the East, Reiner Pilz, planned to build a factory to produce compact discs. He had formed a joint venture with the old East German computer and office equipment manufacturer Robotron VEB in 1989. But Suhl's town council voted against the compact disc factory, saying that the building site in question was too close to a rifle range used to train Olympic athletes.

Bruno Endter read about the Suhl council's rejection of the Pilz-Robotron factory in the local paper and saw an opportunity. Endter is the mayor of Albrechts bei Suhl, a village (pop. 1,000) about five miles from Suhl. He called up a Robotron executive he knew who was originally from Albrechts, and said that maybe his town could provide a building site. "At the time I hadn't even thought about a specific site, only that we should try to do something," says Endter. In March 1990, a few weeks after the Suhl town council rejected the initial site, Pilz and Robotron executives were walking the new site in the hills above Albrechts.

Reiner Pilz is a charismatic presence, a tall, imposing man in his late forties with a thick black mustache and balding head. He first attracted media attention when he developed a fully automated machine to produce compact discs in 1988, and a year later he made headlines with his announcement of the first joint venture with an East German firm. Much of the foreign press, including *The New York Times, Time* magazine and others, has written him up as well.

Reiner Pilz was born in Zwickau in 1942, but unlike Eberhard
Pilz, he was not interested in trying to change the East German
system. He moved to the West before the Wall was built, and
studied construction engineering. He then spent several years
working for a West German construction firm, then a steel company, before founding his own construction company in 1972.

His Pilz Metall & Glas GmbH excelled in steel and glass façades, the mirrored kind that lets people inside the building see
out but not vice versa. With its emphasis on quality, R. Pilz's
company won several notable contracts, including the façade
adorning the Saudi Arabian king's palace in Jedda. Actually, an
Italian firm underbid R. Pilz to win the contract initially, but the
Italians could not live up to the contractual provisions. The façade
had to be able to withstand the fire from the small cannons used
to defend the palace. The Italians figured they'd build the façade,
collect the money and no one would be the wiser. Instead, the
king fired a round at the façade, the façade crumbled and in came
R. Pilz to do the job right.

In the 1980s R. Pilz noticed the exponential growth in the use
of compact discs and thought he might apply his company's technological know-how in producing them. Applying a thin alumi-
num coating to a plastic disc was, after all, quite similar to the
technology used to mirror-coat the glass used in façades. Along
with his brother-in-law Jürgen Haak, an experienced machine
builder, R. Pilz had a team of employees build a fully automated
production system. After some of the initial kinks were worked
out, the machine was capable of producing discs that were 95
percent error free, drastically reducing the cost of production (at
the time the norm for most producers was closer to 75 percent
error free—now they have all improved).

The major compact disc producers like Sony and Philips-
DuPont were hardly enamored with the upstart R. Pilz. They
tried a price war, slashing the price of a disc from DM 7 to around
DM 2.50, but while they lost money in the process, R. Pilz remained profitable. The price war soon stopped. The big guns then
used their marketing muscle to discourage the major record companies from using Pilz discs. That's one reason you won't find
Herbert von Karajan conducting the Vienna Philharmonic or Mi-

chael Jackson singing on a Pilz disc. You will, however, find Telly Savalas of Kojak fame crooning "Love Is Such a Sweet Surprise" or "You're the Closest Thing I've Found to Love" on the Pilz label. Even more successful than the singing Kojak, however, is the Pilz "Vienna Master Series." These discs consist of little-known orchestras and musicians from Eastern Europe playing Bach, Beethoven and other classics. Through his own production and through deals with independent music producers, R. Pilz rapidly reached capacity at his compact disc factory in Kranzberg near Munich and looked to build new production sites elsewhere.

At his offices in Kranzberg, R. Pilz took a few minutes to talk about his reasons for building in eastern Germany. Sentiment was clearly one. Another is that he likes the long-term prospects for the region. "Since everything is being built from scratch, in several years the region will be one of the most productive in the world. Entrepreneurs investing in eastern Germany for the cheap labor had better stay home. With the right training, the Germans in the East will rapidly close the productivity gap with the West and earn comparable wages. The Americans, English, French are making a mistake by not setting up production in [eastern Germany]."

His long-term optimism is dosed with short-term realism, however. "When I returned there [in 1989], I found that nothing had changed from when I had left. The people there were clueless. Most people had been trained not according to what they wanted to do, but what the government told them to do. The companies were accustomed to getting what they wanted. If they needed a piece of land to build on, the government gave it to them. Our way of doing business was completely foreign to them. They had some old commercial law books lying around from 1935. We had to bring our own books with us. Some of the local press there accused me of being a capitalist since I was not building a kindergarten for the children of the employees."

Building the factory in Albrechts also fits in with R. Pilz's concept that compact disc production is viable anywhere. Thus, along with the Albrechts factory, he is building a third in Spain. In addition to producing discs himself, R. Pilz is also keen on selling ready-to-go factories. From a public relations standpoint, however, the decision to build in Albrechts has given R. Pilz far more notoriety than the eventual creation of 300 jobs would normally warrant.

Most jobs for locals around Albrechts will have to wait until the factory is built in 1992. Construction is almost exclusively in the hands of western contractors (with a few local companies doing subcontracting work). But one already has a feeling of how business will forge bonds between the citizens of East and West. At the construction site one day in July 1991, Bruno Endter is sitting with the contractors around a table outside a prefab shed. The workday has ended, and the eight or so people are drinking beer and shooting the breeze.

Endter is dressed in overall shorts and wearing sandals—being a media celebrity of sorts (his picture even made *The New York Times*) has not changed him. He talks of how glad he is to be able to bring jobs to his village. "Hear, hear," say the builders, who compliment Endter's tenacity and say that without him the project never would have gotten off the ground. They are right. Ownership of the building site was divided among some 360 names. "Some of the entries in the register dated back to the 1800s," says Endter. But Albrechts being a small village, Endter was able to track down all the people still alive and persuade them to sell. One woman donated her parcel for nothing. By acting quickly, the Pilz builders and Endter got the approval to build within a matter of months. "In West Germany, it could have taken years to get all the necessary zoning permits, environmental impact statements, et cetera," says Waldemar Knoll, who oversees all the Pilz company building projects. Quietly aside, Knoll admits that building in Spain is even easier than anywhere in Germany: "Everything is more relaxed there."

More beer is drunk, and the empty bottles pile up on the table in true German fashion. The talk turns to the excellent quality of the local Thüringen mustard, and then one of the builders tells of how years ago in the West he came across Thüringen sausages. They were made in West Germany, he says, but they tasted fabulous and the recipe was originally from Thüringen. The underlying message is of no small importance: Germany may have been divided by a barbed-wire fence, but the memory of a common culture lived on in sausage links. For all of East Germany's attempts to create a separate German identity, more unites the Germans than divides them. As Eberhard Pilz of Transmercur in Leipzig predicts, within five years the Germans in the East and the West will be alike—envious, anxious to keep their houses as nice as their neighbors' and mowing the lawn to perfection.

In terms of entrepreneurial drive, little separates Eberhard and Reiner Pilz. The difference is that Reiner Pilz has the means to put that entrepreneurial drive to work. Not to take anything away: in the compact disc business, he is David against the Goliaths like Sony, Philips, Bertelsmann and others (overall he ranks sixth in terms of production). He does not try to sign high-priced pop stars for his label and counts on succeeding through technical superiority, selling his pressing capacity to the "major" music companies. But he has had the chance to build an asset base in a capitalist economy. When the banks balked at financing his share of the DM 250 million investment for the factory in Albrechts, R. Pilz was able to mortgage his Kranzberg headquarters. Risky, perhaps, but he at least had something. And by starting from scratch, he was in the enviable position of being able to hire only the number of people needed.

Eberhard Pilz, on the other hand, was saddled with an inefficient trucking operation, no collateral, a market that overwhelmingly favors his large western competitors and not the slightest hope of finding any venture capital. A bright person who knew enough to get advice from the West, E. Pilz was nevertheless doomed by circumstances to fail at Transmercur. He will no doubt land on his feet elsewhere. But as massive unemployment condemns many Germans in the newly reunited East to despair, the success of local entrepreneurs like Eberhard Pilz cannot come soon enough.

12

Across the Border:
German Business in the World

According to the currently fashionable neo-Clausewitzian formula, economic competition is a continuation of war by other means, where victory is measured by market share rather than territorial gains on the battlefield. If that's the case, then German business, with its outsized export success and elaborate corporate defenses, must be seen as a formidable economic competitor indeed.

But can it be said that German business is fighting to rule the world, or even Europe? Not, I believe, on any conscious level. Despite appearances to the contrary, German business appears by and large to be out to cooperate, not to dominate. As Bernd Stecher, the head of external relations at Siemens, says, "It's one thing to have high exports . . . and another to get along with people in the world and have them take part in development." Stecher's point may sound like mere public relations, but it does seem to reflect the prevailing view in German business circles. Of course, German soft-pedaling of their international business success should not lull anyone into thinking that they are not fierce competitors as well.

For all their economic success, the Germans are extremely unwilling to be cast in the role of economic aggressor. In part it's a historical issue: the Germans, justly or unjustly, were blamed for World War I; without question they were responsible for World War II. The last thing they want is to be placed in the chair of the accused yet again, even if the contention concerns nonlethal matters such as high interest and trade surpluses.

For the time being, the role of economic villain seems safely Japan's to play. The Japanese have virtually taken over entire industries like electronics and semiconductors and grabbed an ever-increasing share of the all-important automobile market. The Japanese trade surplus with the United States, over $40 billion in recent years, has been far more destabilizing than any German surplus. Still, the Germans would prefer not to take chances.

Germany at Large in the World

In keeping with their nonaggressive stance, Germans eagerly portray themselves as Europeans every chance they get. During a 1991 television interview with French journalists, Helmut Kohl responded to praise for the German apprenticeship system with the suggestion that other European countries adopt the German system—then one could speak of the marvelous "European" apprenticeship system. When Germany's lax export controls came under fire in the wake of the 1991 Gulf War, the Germans were quick to point out that France and other European countries had also sold weapons to Iraq, and that "European" export controls were needed. To some extent, Germany's interest in a unified

Europe is driven as much by the desire to deflect resentment against Germany as it is to benefit from a bigger market or a chance to spread the German way of business.

The traditional relationship between German business and the world has begun to shift as well. German companies used to manufacture mostly at home, only then exporting their products beyond their borders. While this arrangement has done wonders for jobs and prosperity at home, the perennial trade surpluses have not always gone over well in countries struggling with trade deficits and less prosperous economies than Germany's. In the past few years, however, more and more German companies have stepped up their direct foreign investments and in the process have taken on more of a multinational character. While trade and investment statistics reflect this trend, spotting the changes on the ground hasn't been quite so easy. The Germans usually do not like to announce their arrival with trumpet flourishes.

In 1986 Frankenthal-based KSB AG, the leading German (and European) maker of pumps and valves for heavy industry, merged with the leading French (and second-largest European) pump manufacturer, Pompes Guinard SA. Few people paid much attention to the low-profile merger, which suited the typically privacy-minded German company just fine.

Since the merger, KSB's revenues have grown to more than DM 2 billion, making the company the world leader in its market and a formidable competitor of American companies such as Dresser and Ingersoll Rand as well as of the Japanese manufacturer Ebara. A solid majority of the publicly traded KSB is owned by Klein Pumpen GmbH, which is in turn 99 percent owned by a private foundation. No fear of takeovers in Frankenthal.

In merging with Pompes Guinard, KSB looked to become the undisputed European leader. A further goal was to build a binational company—albeit one governed from Germany—and not simply to eliminate a competitor or cherry-pick the best divisions. A seat on both the KSB management and supervisory boards was given to the French; the company also restructured itself into eight divisions, with each division headed indiscriminately by either a French or a German manager (it happens that most are, for the time being, German). And most divisions consist of at least two plants, one in France and one in Germany.

What KSB shows is how a German company can position itself well for a burgeoning Europe in the 1990s without too obviously playing the role of the heavy. The Franco-German management structure currently favors the Germans, but this unique structure also suggests that the path to the top can be taken by either French or Germans (or perhaps other nationals). At the same time, KSB benefits from a typically German ownership structure that virtually eliminates the possibility of takeovers. Management is free to concentrate on building on its world-leading market share over the long term, and not to worry about quarterly dividends.

KSB remains typically German in another way: its will to privacy. Hubertus von Münchhausen, head of the company's public relations department, did not wish to see his company featured in a book destined for American readers: "Some of our biggest competitors are in America, and they might find out how we do so well." Reminded that KSB is nominally a public company and that surely shareholders are entitled to know something about the company, von Münchhausen replied, "We have one main shareholder, with whom we deal directly." He was, of course, referring to the company's controlling foundation, conveniently ignoring any pesky minority shareholders who would dare to ask for information about a company in which they had invested.

The International Background

While some observers outside Germany, seeing more and more companies like KSB investing internationally, might cry out, "The Germans are coming!" they should remember that in one sense German companies are only making up lost ground. Quite a few budding German multinationals were nipped by historical circumstances earlier this century.

The electrical giant Siemens was very active in both England and Russia soon after its founding in 1847; the tsar, for example, had commissioned what was then known as the Siemens & Halske telegraph company to link St. Petersburg with Odessa so that he could be kept abreast of developments in the Crimean War. In England, where industrialization was already far advanced, Siemens did brisk business selling electrical equipment. Both markets disappeared during World War I.

The American Bosch Magneto Company, an early subsidiary of Robert Bosch's namesake company, was established on West Fifty-sixth Street in New York several years before World War I. The company sold spark plugs, both imported from Germany and manufactured at a small plant in Springfield, Massachusetts. Then the United States entered the war, Congress passed the 1917 Alien Property Act and Bosch saw its U.S. business expropriated.

Merck, Inc., based in Rahway, New Jersey, is currently the world's leading pharmaceuticals company. Prior to World War I, however, the American company was a subsidiary of the Darm-stadt-based company that today is known as E. Merck oHG. Since then, Merck, Inc., has gone on to dwarf its lost parent; at last count the New Jersey–based company had sales of over $7 billion, while E. Merck, held privately by the descendants of the founding Merck family, quietly chalks up respectable sales of over DM 3.5 billion.

German business took a long time to recover from the losses incurred as a result of World War I. The international activities of German companies remained limited right through World War II, and during the early postwar period, reconstruction kept German companies busy at home. Capital flowed mostly into Germany, not out. The deutsche mark established itself as a premier currency only after several decades, so foreign investments were costly for German firms early on. And German firms preferred to manufacture with their highly skilled domestic labor force; to this day the absence of skilled labor abroad, at least as the Germans define the term, acts as a brake on more German foreign investment.

It wasn't until the mid-1970s that German foreign investments began to outpace money entering Germany, a trend that continues today. Still, the Germans have yet to strike fear into the hearts of other nations with their buying habits, at least not the way the Americans did for decades after World War II, or the way the Japanese do now.

After World War II left the European economies in ruins, the field was wide open for IBM, Coca-Cola, Procter & Gamble and countless other American companies to establish dominant positions overseas. Some Europeans, like the French intellectual Jean-Jacques Servan-Schreiber in his widely acclaimed book *Le Défi américain,* wondered if European companies could meet so powerful a challenge from the Americans. Ultimately, the answer was yes. Over time, European countries prospered and the American advantage was slowly eroded. American companies still enjoy strong overseas positions, but today the threat is for the most part gone. Or rather, a new threat has emerged.

In the last decade, Japan has almost completely replaced the United States as international bogeyman. In the automobile industry, to cite the most salient example, Japanese car and car parts manufacturers have used direct investments in the United States, and to a lesser degree in Europe, to secure and build market share which the Japanese firms had originally gained through regular exports. Just how far the Japanese can go remains up in the air, but American and European automakers naturally fear that their own competitive positions will get a lot worse before they get better. And what has been true for the auto industry, the line goes, may also come to pass in other industries as well: microelectronics, computers.

By comparison, fears that "the Germans are coming" should be taken in context. German companies keep investing more and more outside the country, but just as German firms do not dominate specific industries through exports, neither will they do so through foreign investment. And the Germans still have a lot of catching up to do. In the United States, for example, Germany trails Britain, Japan, the Netherlands and Canada in overall foreign investment.

The International Market

If German firms have begun to come out from behind their rocks to invest more abroad, the reasons tend to be market related. Typically, businesses want to ensure access to the host country's market, not simply benefit from their lower wage costs.

For years, the Bosch Group has been heavily concentrated in Germany: foreign assets account for 25 percent or less of the company's total. Lately, though, the auto parts manufacturer has been strengthening its overseas presence. In the United States, Bosch invested heavily in its "Made in America" image—partially out of fear that Congress might pass "local content" legislation for the automobile industry. In Britain, Bosch does not have to fear protectionism, but the firm recently invested nearly DM 500 million in Wales to build an alternator assembly plant. There the Germans want to keep up with Japanese manufacturers such as Toyota and Nissan, which are concentrating their European investments in Britain.

German foreign investment has also been driven by the logical desire to be present in all of the world's major markets, especially the United States. The media company Bertelsmann AG, for example, shelled out nearly $1 billion to acquire RCA records and Doubleday publishing in the United States in 1986. The Allianz insurance company spent almost $3 billion in 1990 to buy the Fireman's Fund property and casualty insurance company in the United States.

Constricting regulation at home also drives German companies to invest abroad. The German chemical concern BASF AG calculated that tough domestic pollution control regulations will cost the firm up to DM 300 million a year by 1993. In a good year, that figure represents the company's total reinvested profits. No wonder BASF management is looking to shift more of its production abroad, where regulations may not be so costly. In 1990, almost 50 percent of the firm's investments were made outside Germany, compared to around 33 percent ten years earlier.

Although German investment and trade statistics show increased activity within the EC during the past several years, Germans are not looking to create a "Fortress Europe" trade bloc. Germany wants and needs free trade around the globe, and no point on the globe remains too remote for the German businessman. As Fritz Mayer pointed out in Chapter 3, he would fly to Asia for the day if that's what it took to sell one of his company's textile machines there.

German companies typically spare no expense or effort when breaking into a new market. Without a vast internal market like that of the United States, the Germans have to be tenacious exporters in order to succeed. Consider BMW's experience in Japan. When the makers of the "ultimate driving machine" decided to break into the ultimate controlled market in the early 1980s, the

Munich-based company devoted more than five times the normal resources to the cause. The effort paid off as BMW grabbed the largest market share of any luxury car importer. From his office in the Tokyo suburb of Chiba City, the head of BMW-Japan, Hans Peter Sonnenborn, explained the secrets of BMW's success (he has since moved on to Audi).

"The success is relative, since we only have .8 percent of the market. But because Japan is Japan, where foreign importers combined only have 4 percent of the market, it's fair to speak of relative success. In the beginning, we went about business as though we were selling twenty or thirty thousand cars, not two or three thousand [today the company sells more than 35,000 cars annually through more than 120 dealers]. We geared the resources —advertising costs a lot here—to the market potential, not the actual market. We started early on to work with our engineers in Germany to equip the cars for the Japanese market. Here there is more stop-and-go traffic and hotter weather, so we used different brakes and bigger cooling systems. We invested a lot in after-sales service. If the buyer of a seven-series car is stranded somewhere because his car broke down, we pick up the hotel bill.

"But the determining factor for BMW was that we set up our own dealer network. That was difficult, especially in the beginning. The land was extremely expensive, and the best locations had already been taken. But today, although we're at a disadvantage compared to the Japanese dealers, we have an advantage over the other importers who were later into the market. Having our own dealership network allowed us to use our own marketing techniques without any interference or compromise."

A tight control over the marketing in Japan proved to be essential. German-made luxury cars can cost anywhere from 10 percent to 30 percent more than equivalent Japanese luxury cars such as the Acura Legend. "You need a strong brand," says Sonnenborn. "We were able to build our own showrooms here, which have the same distinctive look around the world. The Japanese buyers are very status conscious. It's not so much like in the United States, where you're considered clever for buying cheaply. The Japanese feel that if they pay more, they are getting better quality."

Sonnenborn and BMW have obviously done something right.

Whereas in the United States BMW has lost considerable market share to Japanese cars like the Acura Legend, the Germans are competing nicely on the Japanese manufacturers' home turf. Is there a lesson here for U.S. manufacturers? Indeed there is, according to Sonnenborn: "The American producers hide behind their government and complain that they cannot be successful here because they cannot get into the Japanese distribution system. I say, so what? Build your own. If you are in an industry that supplies other Japanese industries, that may not be possible. But it is when you sell a product like cars directly to the consumer.

"Furthermore, it doesn't help if the Americans force the Japanese carmakers to give up their exclusive arrangements with their dealers. That would mean we would have to give up ours. Then the Japanese will be officially nonexclusive, but unofficially, they will still have control over their dealers. The only people who will lose out are us.

"Look at Honda. In a prefecture where they have ten or twelve dealers, there's a staff of thirty-five Honda people who watch over their dealers. In the same prefecture we have ten or twelve dealers, but only one BMW person watching them. We have good communications, but also we trust our dealer to make his own decisions. If the exclusive relationship were gone, we'd lose our influence over our dealers, but Honda would not. Thus the American efforts to open the market are a strike against us. None of the Americans have done what we did. They hide behind their noses. Now they realize they could have done more, and they cry to their government for help."

Sonnenborn's point about the Americans was illustrated in near-farcical fashion when George Bush took leading American automobile executives with him on an official visit to Japan in 1992. These same executives have refused to make cars with the steering wheel on the right for the Japanese market. For its Japanese exports, BMW not only puts the steering wheel on the right (a point Sonnenborn does not even feel the need to mention because it goes without saying), but redesigns the cooling systems and brakes as well.

The future success of BMW in Japan is certainly not a given.

Japanese car buyers may soon decide that the status associated with owning a BMW is not worth the higher price. But in the meantime, the Germans have taken the high ground among the importers in the Japanese luxury car market, a market that has, according to Sonnenborn, only recently been opened to competition: "Between 1985 and 1988 the Japanese got rid of the various nontariff barriers, and the tax reform in 1989 meant that many of our cars were no longer penalized."

The example of BMW in Japan demands attention because everyone knows the German cars and the tough reputation of the Japanese market. More often, though, the German export success story is more discreet. As Harvard Business School professor Michael Porter points out in his brick of a book, *The Competitive Advantage of Nations,* "German firms to not dominate industries the way U.S. and Japanese companies do." But, adds Porter, "no country in the world, including Japan, exhibits the breadth and depth of industries with strong international positions." Porter cites statistics showing how German firms have snared at least 30 percent of the world export market in everything from coal briquettes to potassium sulfate, pumps, fresh milk, printing presses, jukeboxes, rubber and plastics machines, packaging machines, sewing machine needles, textile machines—the list is long.

As Porter's list shows, German companies tend to be invisible because they are strong in industries not visible to consumers. Who would know that 90 percent of all lace in the United States is made on a Karl Mayer GmbH machine, or that a Budweiser label is stuck on thanks to a bottle-labeling machine from Krones AG?

With the notable exception of the automobile industry, few German companies have succeeded in maintaining international brands. Either the Germans fail to keep up with consumer tastes, or their advertising fails them. Adidas, once the best-known name in sneakers and athletic wear, was sold by the Dassler family to Frenchman Bernard Tapie. Braun, well known for appliances such as coffee grinders and electric shavers, is now owned by Gillette; Löwenbräu sold the license to brew its beer in the United States to Miller, part of Philip Morris. But the lack of strong brands has obviously not hurt Germany's overall export record.

It would be well to keep in mind those industries in which
Germany holds so large an international market share. Protesta-
tions notwithstanding, the Germans are indeed coming, if only
by default.

The International Presence at Home

For all of Germany's strength in exports and, more recently, in
foreign investment, German business cannot be considered a de-
stabilizing force in the world economy. Trade and investment go
both ways, and while there are occasionally instances of German
protectionism (name a country entirely free of them), the country,
by and large, is open.

Critics can always point to those few industries—coal, shipbuilding, aerospace—that receive government subsidies. And yes,
German telecommunications has been a government monopoly
for years, and German utilities have a virtual lock on the domestic
power market. But not everyone in German business supports
these obstacles to free competition, and many of them are sched-
uled to be reduced soon anyway. More important, a look at the
broader picture reveals that the German economy is in fact wide
open.

Overall, Germany has more assets in foreign hands (17 percent) than does the United States (8 percent) and a great deal more
than Japan (1 percent). The ranks of the thirty largest German
industrial corporations according to 1990 sales include subsidiaries
of GM, Ford, IBM, Shell, Exxon and Unilever. Germans may be
famous for their cars, but both GM, through its Adam Opel AG
subsidiary, and Ford Germany sell more passenger cars in Germany than do either Mercedes-Benz or BMW (only Volkswagen
sells more than the American subsidiaries). Foreign companies
obviously can and do succeed in Germany.

The problem for German business is that, as every investment
prospectus warns, past performance does not guarantee future
results. Today, German business has a relaxed attitude—to put it
kindly—toward attracting foreign investment. The assumption in
German business circles seems to be that Germany has always
been open to foreign investment and that foreign companies will
naturally want to do business in Europe's premier economy. The

notion is partially true. In 1989, the year the Berlin Wall fell, overall foreign investment growth in Germany jumped by more than 13 percent, double the growth rate of previous years.

But Germany is not exactly an easy market to break into, given the high costs and tough competition. The corporate tax rate is anywhere from 10 percent to 15 percent higher than the European norm. Telecommunications are inordinately expensive. Labor costs are high, and working hours are short. Yes, higher German productivity compensates for some of those high costs, but the first-time investor cannot be sure of that. Furthermore, with the advent of a supposedly barrier-free European Community beginning in 1993, the incentive to invest in Germany becomes even further reduced. Statistics compiled by the American Chamber of Commerce in Germany show, for example, that in the latter half of the 1980s, the investment growth of American and Japanese firms was greater in Britain and the Netherlands than in Germany.

The Germans are not deliberately trying to discourage foreign investment—the country's powerful antitakeover provisions, for example, are only a small piece of a large picture. But the well-established foreign firms doing business in Germany broke into the market long ago. Ford first went to Germany in the mid-1920s, while General Motors took control of Opel in 1929. Others invested soon after the war, when costs were less prohibitive. These companies, which are very well accepted by the Germans, thrive in Germany. In the case of Opel, the American subsidiary even "out-Germaned" a lot of other German companies with its swift decision to invest in the newly reunified East. In Eisenach, just a few miles over the former East German border, Opel is building a highly modernized car assembly factory that, it is claimed, will rival Japanese plants for productivity.

For more recent foreign investors, though, acceptance by the German business community can sometimes take a while. Germans are not xenophobic, but they do want to see that the foreigner will maintain a strong sense of social responsibility, not just try to make a quick buck. Robert Holdheim of the American Chamber of Commerce in Germany mentions how for an American or any other foreign newcomer, "there is a certain degree of being left out of things like standards bodies, government contact circles and industry associations. You take a company like Motorola, which has been in Germany for about 25 years now and is just starting to be accepted." A spokeswoman for Motorola's German subsidiary would only say that the company considers itself German.

Still, determined companies will continue to invest in Germany. For all of the country's barriers of cost, social responsibility and highly rationalized organization, Germany remains an eminently pregnable fortress, with lots of fertile ground inside. The German market does, after all, offer political stability, wealthy consumers, few disruptive labor strikes, good infrastructure, skilled labor and the knowledge that, as Frank Sinatra might sing, "if I can make it there, I'll make it anywhere." Any company that can satisfy the quality-obsessed German consumers and still turn a profit is doing something right.

In the short term, however, Germany could do more to attract foreign investment. Government officials and executives from the Treuhandanstalt have lobbied in the United States and Japan for investment in eastern Germany, for example, but the conditions there are hardly inspiring. Most of the high costs of doing business in Germany—wages, telecommunications, taxes—have been swiftly transposed to the East, while the advantages of the German market—high productivity, good infrastructure—have not yet been put into place. That's not to say that eastern Germany will not develop into a good market over time. Chances are it will. But if the Germans seriously want to attract new foreign investment in a hurry, they will have to make it still easier.

Conclusion

The spectacular rise of German business from the rubble of World War II has quite naturally engendered admiration, envy and, in some cases, criticism.

It may appear, looking through American eyes, that some facets of the inner workings of Germany's business culture are weak or even misguided. Germans often seem excessively inflexible to outsiders. Their byzantine network of corporate crossholdings smacks of a conspiratorial insularity offensive to American notions of free enterprise and openness. So do the power and conservatism of Germany's banks. Can Germany continue to attract foreign investment in such an atmosphere, and with the cost of doing business there so high? Will such costs eventually price Germany's products and services out of the international market? It's always a possibility.

Yet any doubts about Germany's capacity to survive and flourish in the next few decades pale in comparison with Germany's many strengths. Beyond the obvious—a tradition of quality, a highly skilled and happy labor force, growing capital markets and a powerful group of middle-size industrial firms—Germany's greatest strength may be its canny, sophisticated approach to the world outside its boundaries. The sort of disparaging remarks recently made by assorted Japanese politicians about the United States—its best customer—would never be heard on the lips of their German counterparts. And Germany's role in Europe, both East and West, bears close attention: in addition to possessing the continent's strongest economy and a privileged position at its geographical center, Germany was the first to recognize the diplomatic status of a divided Yugoslavia—a clear sign of its growing political leadership in Europe. At the same time, Germany is willing to give up some of its insularity, its economic autonomy, for an even greater role in the leadership of Europe. For the Germans the benefits will no doubt outweigh the costs.

The point is that the United States can no longer afford to concentrate all its energies on "doing something" about Japan; we ignore Germany at our peril. I am not advocating Germany-bashing any more than I support Japan-bashing. But I do believe that Germany's many strengths, coupled with its sophistication, will land it sooner or later in a position we will no longer be able to ignore. We should prepare ourselves.

One way to prepare would be to consider carefully all the features of German business that have made Germany so successful. It's perhaps a little too easy—and not very useful—to take potshots at the United States for not being more like Germany. After all, we aren't like Germany, and we do have strengths—our geography, our natural resources, our innovative spirit and entrepreneurial drive—that Germany either can never or may never acquire. But our absolute commitment to an illusory free market does us no good when at the same time we ignore such fundamentals as improving our educational system and the basic skills of our labor force. The German economic model, with its strong emphasis on social concerns, works. Will Germany succeed in raising to western levels the economic and social conditions in its newly reunited eastern regions? Yes. Not without problems along the way, but I suspect the Germans will have succeeded long before Americans have raised the economic and social conditions in their inner cities to acceptable levels.

One final word. In doing the research for this book, I had the pleasure to speak with many Germans of all ages. There still exists among most Germans tremendous goodwill toward Americans. To be sure, the growing influence of Germany in Europe may occasionally lead to differences with America in economic and political matters, but the bonds that unite the two cultures will not easily be broken.

GLOSSARY

The following list explains some of the terms that appear in this book and is intended for easy reference. Terms are also explained in the text.

Types of Companies

Aktiengesellschaft, or **AG,** is a stock corporation. Most are publicly traded, but they need not be.

Gesellschaft mit beschränkter Haftung, or **GmbH,** is a privately held, limited liability corporation.

Kommanditgesellschaft, or **KG,** is a limited partnership.

Kommanditgesellschaft auf Aktien, or **KGaA,** is a limited partnership that also has shares which may or may not be publicly quoted.

Offene Handelsgesellschaft, or **oHG,** is a general partnership.

GmbH and Co., KG, is a limited partnership (the KG) whose general partner is a limited liability corporation (the GmbH).

Volkseigener Betrieb, or **VEB,** was the term for the East German state-owned corporations prior to reunification. Thereafter, each VEB was either transformed into an AG or a GmbH by the Treuhandanstalt, or else shut down altogether.

Company Terms

Aufsichtsrat is a company's supervisory board, much like a board of directors.

Vorstand is a management board, which includes a company's chief executive along with other top executives. No one from the management board may serve on the same company's supervisory board.

Betriebsrat is an employee council, consisting of elected representatives from the work force. These councils work with management to oversee internal company matters.

Mitbestimmung, or codetermination, applies to all large companies (as defined by the number of employees, assets or sales volume), and consists of giving elected employee representatives seats on the company's supervisory board. The German coal and steel industry is subject to its own set of codetermination rules.

Arbeitsdirektor is a management board position, created under the rules of codetermination, whose holder is responsible for employee matters. In the coal and steel industry, labor and management have to agree on the candidate. In other industries, management may use its own discretion.

Associations and Other Entities

Treuhandanstalt, or **Treuhand,** is the German government's privatization agency charged with selling off the old East German state-owned companies.

Bundesverband der Deutschen Industrie, or **BDI,** is a large industrial association whose leadership is culled from the ranks of top German executives and whose members are other industrial associations. Activities include economic and business research as well as lobbying.

Deutscher Industrie- und Handelstag, or **DIHT,** is the umbrella organization for the local chambers of commerce. Activities include economic research and lobbying.

Technischer Überwachungsverein, or **TÜV,** is a technical supervisory association. Virtually every German federal state has a TÜV, which performs quality control and consulting work and ensures compliance with technical regulations.

Industriegewerkschaft, or **IG,** is an industry union. The "IG" is typically used as a prefix, as in "IG Metall" for the metalworkers' union.

Deutscher Gewerkschaftsbund, or **DGB,** is an umbrella organization for German unions.

Allgemeine Ortskrankenkasse, or **AOK,** is a regional health insurance fund. All Germans with salaries below a certain level must belong, while those with higher salaries may choose private health insurance.

Staatssicherheitsdienst, or **Stasi,** is the now defunct secret police of East Germany.

Political Parties

Christlich-Demokratische Union, or **CDU,** is the Christian Democratic party, which is on the right.

Freie Demokratische Partei, or **FDP,** is the Free Democratic party, a centrist party. The CDU and FDP have combined to form the ruling conservative coalition since 1982.

Sozialdemokratische Partei Deutschlands, or **SPD,** is the Social Democratic party, which is on the left.

Partei des Demokratischen Sozialismus, or **PDS,** is the Party of Democratic Socialism, the reincarnated version of East Germany's Communist party after reunification.

BIBLIOGRAPHY

The following works were either referred to, quoted from or drawn upon for this book.

Albert, Michel. *Capitalisme contre capitalisme* (Capitalism against capitalism). Paris: Seuil, 1991.

Blundell, William E. "A Modest Proposal." *Wall Street Journal,* April 18, 1990.

Burstein, Daniel. *Euroquake: Europe's Explosive Economic Challenge Will Change the World.* New York: Simon and Schuster, 1991.

Büschemann, Karl-Heinz. "Vorstoß ins Leere" (Exploring the Unknown). *Die Zeit,* April 12, 1991.

Decker, Hans. "Master Craftsman, No College Required." *Wall Street Journal,* March 18, 1991.

Eglau, Hans Otto. *Erste Garnitur: Die Mächtigen der deutschen Wirtschaft* (The Cream of the Crop: The powerful in German business). Düsseldorf and Vienna: Econ Verlag GmbH, 1980.

————. *Wie Gott in Frankfurt: Die Deutsche Bank und die deutsche Industrie* (Godlike in Frankfurt: The Deutsche Bank and German industry). Düsseldorf and Vienna: Econ Verlag GmbH, 1989.

Fröbe, Rainer. "Der Arbeitseinsatz von KZ-Häftlingen und die Perspektive der Industrie, 1943–1945" (The forced labor of concentration camp prisoners and the perspective of industry, 1943–1945). In Herbert, Ulrich, ed., *Europa und der "Reichseinsatz"* (Europe and the forced labor of the Third Reich). Essen: Klartext Verlag, 1991.

Gérard, Florence. "Bonjour, Herr Dr. . . ." *Lettre de la rue Saint Guillaume,* February 1990.

Hamilton, Stephen F. *Apprenticeship for Adulthood: Preparing Youth for the Future.* New York: The Free Press, 1990.

Herbert, Ulrich. "Nicht Entschädigungsfähig? Die Wiedergutmachungsansprüche der Ausländer" (Not fit for compensation? The reparations claims of foreigners). In Herbst, Ludolf, and Constantin Goschler, eds., *Wiedergutmachung in der Bundesrepublik Deutschland* (Reparations in the Federal Republic of Germany). Munich: R. Oldenbourg Verlag GmbH, 1989.

Hessdörfer, Karl. "Die finanzielle Dimension" (The financial dimension). In Herbst, Ludolf, and Constantin Goschler, eds., *Wiedergutmachung in der Bundesrepublik Deutschland* (Reparations in the Federal Republic of Germany). Munich: R. Oldenbourg Verlag GmbH, 1989.

Heuss, Theodor. *Robert Bosch: Leben und Leistung* (Robert Bosch:

Life and achievement). Tübingen: Rainer Wunderlich Verlag, Hermann Leins, 1946.

Kuttner, Robert. *The End of Laissez-Faire: National Purpose and the Global Economy after the Cold War*. New York: Alfred A. Knopf, 1990.

Langbein, Hermann. "Entschädigung für KZ-Häftlinge? Ein Erfahrungsbericht" (Compensation for concentration camp prisoners? A case history). In Herbst, Ludolf, and Constantin Goschler, eds., *Wiedergutmachung in der Bundesrepublik Deutschland* (Reparations in the Federal Republic of Germany). Munich: R. Oldenbourg Verlag GmbH, 1989.

Leyendecker, Hans, and Richard Rickelmann. *Exporteure des Todes: Deutscher Rüstungsskandal in Nahost* (Exporters of death: German armaments scandal in the Middle East). Göttingen: Steidl Verlag, 1990.

Linden, Dana Wechsler, with Vicki Contavespi. "Incentivize Me, Please." *Forbes,* May 27, 1991.

Michaels, James. "Nervous Prosperity." *Forbes,* July 8, 1991.

Mohn, Reinhard. *Success Through Partnership: An Entrepreneurial Strategy*. New York: Doubleday, 1986.

Otto, Werner. *Die Otto Gruppe: Der Weg zum Großunternehmen* (The Otto Group: The road to a large corporation). Düsseldorf and Vienna: Econ Verlag GmbH, 1982.

Pfaff, William. "American Pauperization Was Not Part of the Bargain." *International Herald Tribune,* December 6, 1991.

Porter, Michael E. *The Competitive Advantage of Nations*. New York: The Free Press, 1990.

Servan-Schreiber, Jean-Jacques. *Le Défi américain* (The American challenge). Paris: Denoël, 1967.

Staguhn, Gerhard. "Wo der frühe Kapitalismus überlebte" (Where early capitalism survived). *Frankfurter Allgemeine Zeitung,* April 12, 1991.

Wallraf, Rudolf, and Richard Rickelmann. "Die Pistole auf den Tisch gelegt (The pistol on the table). *Der Spiegel,* December 3, 1990.

Wechsler, Dana. "Just Deserts." *Forbes,* May 28, 1990.

Wolf, Christa. *Nachdenken über Christa T.* (Reflections on Christa T.) Halle: Mitteldeutscher Verlag, 1968.

INDEX